# ALL THE KING'S

## *Men*

### ESTABLISHING A NEW KINGDOM

#### BOOK 2

Bishop William A. Lee, Jr.

ISBN 979-8-88992-431-9

All quotes, unless otherwise noted, are taken from The Holy Bible, King James Version. Copyright © 1972 by Thomas Nelson Inc., Camden, New Jersey 08103.

Scriptures marked NKJV are from the New King James Version. Copyright 1979, 1980, 1982 by Thomas Nelson, Inc. Used by permission. All rights reserved.

Scriptures marked NIV are taken from the HOLY BIBLE, NEW INTERNATIONAL VERSION. Copyright © 1973, 1978, 1984 by International Bible Society. Used by permission of Zondervan Publishing House. All rights reserved.

Scriptures marked NAS are taken from the NEW AMERICAN STANDARD BIBLE®, Copyright © 1960, 1962, 1963, 1971, 1972, 1973, 1975, 1977, 1995 by The Lockman Foundation, LaHabra, CA Used by permission. All rights reserved.

Scriptures marked TLB are taken from The Living Bible. Copyright © 1971 by Tyndale House Publishers, Wheaton, Illinois 60187. All rights reserved.

Scriptures marked AMP are taken from The Amplified Bible, containing the amplified Old Testament and the amplified New Testament. 1987. The Lockman Foundation: La Habra, CA Published by permission.

Scriptures marked MSG are taken from The Message Bible, originally published by NavPress in English as THE MESSAGE: The Bible in Contemporary Language copyright 2002 by Eugene Peterson. All rights reserved. (*The Message Bible Online*)

# DEDICATIONS

I would like to dedicate my second book to the following persons who GOD used to touch and bless my life.

First, to my lovely wife Sheila. I am grateful to God for your love and support. As a partner in ministry and a constant woman of prayer, your life and ministry has touched and blessed many.

To the late Uncle Elton and Aunt Cora Williams who have always been a tremendous source of encouragement and wisdom since the days of my youth. Thank you for your love and example, you are truly missed.

To the following persons who trusted me enough to use their positions of influence to create for me a platform to expose the gift that God has given me to the world. The late Bishop Edgar McNeil the Founder and Pastor of Springfield Church of God in Springfield, Massachusets. The late Peter C. Barrett the Founder and Pastor of Rehoboth Church of God, the late Bishop Billy J. O'Neal, Former Church of God Presiding Bishop Robert White, President of Lee University Dr. Paul Conn, The Ministers and Friends of the Church of God Northeast Fellowship and the Pastors and Members of my Church of God home Region of Southern New England.

Special Thanks to Angelia Keinlen of Cleveland, Tennessee and my sister Rachelle Lee of Springfield, Massachusetts, Dr. Lois Burgess, and Dr. Sharon Apopa of Bermuda for all of your work in editing and typing.

To all of my true and special friends who inspire me from day to day. To The Classical High Five (Marcus, Paul, Tommy, Ben and all who have come aboard) Love you My Brothers. Your friendship means more to me than words can express, and I am grateful to the God I serve for blessing me with all of you.

To the wonderful congregation of Victorious Life Church in Conyers, Georgia. You inspire me and are the best Church Family a Pastor can ever have. I Love you!!!

# FOREWORD

How could he ever move beyond being a shepherd boy anyway? David's dad didn't see it in him. His own brothers missed it by a thousand miles. King Saul didn't want to believe it, but God saw "kingness" in him and that's all that mattered.

God began a process of bringing men into David's life that would cultivate and criticize, praise and pulverize, develop and despise. They would serve him, and some would attempt to sacrifice him. Others would acclaim him, while some would attempt to assassinate him. Yet, God used them all to make David the man and the king he became.

William A. Lee, Jr. wrote and described many of David's influencers in his first volume of "All the King's Men." In Volume Two, William digs even deeper to mine the gold and other gems of revelation to show the reader the power of influence in a man's life.

Lee has always been known as a "prince" among preachers. Now, he is quickly establishing his place among tremendous Christian authors, producing well - sought - after material that helps grow Christian character and integrity.

Find a quiet place and settle in with this book. You'll likely read it in one setting, as it captivates your attention, but even more so, your spirit. A prince of preachers is about to take you on a journey with a king who found the heart of God. Who knows, while reading this inspired work, you may even discover that there is a king in you, and you are about to find your place in God's ordained plan.

Tim Hill

Presiding Bishop, Church of God

# CONTENTS

# PREFACE

We will discover in "All the King's Men Book 2" how God used the many relationships that David had during his life's Journey which were both negative and positive to prepare him for his ultimate purpose in life. We need to understand that God desires to take us all to a place of destiny. He wants us to reign in the area in which He has anointed us and in which He has called us to excel. Along the course of that journey, going from here to there, He will allow people to come into our lives as well as remove others from our lives, to work out His purpose in us. Some of these people are good people who will bless us, but then some of these people are not so good people and will cause us pain. David had to transition out of the palace and into his wilderness in order to move to the next level of the process of preparing him to establish a new kingdom and then reign successfully in that new kingdom.

# SECTION ONE
# TRANSITION

Whenever God is about to do something significant, He engages Himself in the art of transitioning those whom He plans to use to their next place of assignment. God, with an eye to and knowledge of the future, begins to move in and around His people. He strategically places them where He desires for them to be and at the time, He wants them to be there. He engages in moving them in and out, opening and closing doors, establishing one and taking down another, connecting us with divinely ordained friendships and loosing us from damaging ones as He, as the Divine Director of the Universe, prepares the set to film the next act in the drama called, Our Lives."

## *Forced Out of the Palace*

And Saul sought to smite David even to the wall with the javelin; but he slipped away out of Saul's presence, and he smote the javelin into the wall; and David fled and escaped that night. (1 Samuel 19:10)

Whenever God is about to do something significant, He engages Himself in the art of transitioning those whom He plans to use to their next place of assignment. With an eye to and knowledge of the future, God begins to move in and around His people. He strategically places them where He desires for them to be and at the time, He wants them to be there. He engages in moving them in and out, opening and closing doors, establishing one and taking down another, connecting us with divinely ordained friendships and loosing us from damaging ones as He, as the Divine Director of the Universe, prepares the set to film the next act in the drama called, "Our Lives."

As people of the kingdom, we would probably not have any problem with God doing this if somehow, we were able to see the end of the script and fully understand what He is doing and why He is doing it. However, we know that God does not work like that. God will often move us without prior notice and without our permission or consultation. He will speak to us to try to move us to that place that He wants us to be. If we do not hear Him or do not move or think we are too comfortable to move, than God will actually cause those who are around us to behave in ways that will leave us without much choice.

**As the Divine Director of the Universe, God prepares the set to film the next act in the drama called, "Our Lives."**

People who were dependable will suddenly start tripping and flipping. People who were trustworthy become untrustworthy. People who loved us change their feelings toward us. It seems as though the very people who invited us into the palace and were agents in transitioning us the last time are suddenly running us out of the palace. The palace is the dwelling place of kings, queens, emperors, and rulers. It represents a place of power and influence. The larger and more fortified a palace is, the greater the defense and the protection that it provides for the king. It stands as a monument to the majesty behind the throne, a place of security and safety as only the most elite soldiers were assigned to guard the gates.

To be allowed entrance into the palace is indeed one of the greatest privileges known to any citizen in that particular kingdom. Oftentimes that type of invitation is only extended to Heads of State, to royalty, and to trusted friends. To actually be invited to live in the palace was an even higher privilege for it was a sign that one was connected and possessed influence with the king, himself. Palace living gave the individual access to the throne of the king. It is nice to be connected to people in high places; to be able to pick up the phone and talk to the right person and have what we need at a moment's notice. To have what we call clout or pull or juice. Because we all know that sometimes it is not what we know but who we know so it is nice to be connected. However, if we are not careful with our connections and our reliance upon them, we can actually get ruined by palace life.

Palace life can spoil us. Although we are connected here on earth, we can find ourselves blindly caught up in compromising our morals, our identity, and our good name. While we are strengthening our earthly connections, we can run the risk of losing our connections with our Heavenly Father. There are times we allow ourselves to become too dependent upon our connections, and then God will allow the hearts of men to turn against us and allow them to be instruments to run us out of the palace. Such was the case for David as the up and down relationship that David had with his surrogate father, Saul the King of all Israel, develops into an attempt on David's life.

One of the interesting things about this relationship is that Saul actually hates David for absolutely no reason. If one looks at the actions of David, we will find that David actually did everything that Saul desired him to do. He was even brave enough to take on some of his enemies and fight some of his battles when Saul was not interested in fighting, such as the battle David fought with Goliath the Giant from Gath. Instead of receiving and appreciating David, Saul was overcome by his own insecurities and behaved like he was intoxicated with hatred. Instead of embracing David, Saul became afraid of him.

And Saul was afraid of David, because the LORD was with him, and was departed from Saul. Therefore, Saul removed him from him, and made him his captain over a thousand; and he went out and came in before the people. And David behaved himself wisely in all his ways; and the LORD was with him. Wherefore when Saul saw that he behaved himself very wisely, he was afraid of him. **(1 Samuel 18:12-15)**

The Bible says Saul was afraid of David because the Lord was with him and the Spirit of God had departed from Saul. Therefore, Saul removed him from the palace and made him his captain over thousands. David behaved wisely and the Lord was with him. I suggest that much of the consternation and hatred that is directed toward us by certain individuals is due to the fact that those individuals are insecure within themselves and are actually threatened by our spirit of excellence. No matter what we do or how much we tell them we love them and are on their side, it doesn't seem to make any difference. Once they have made up their minds about us, most likely their minds will never change.

You can encourage that co-worker, you can slave for that boss, you can prove yourself faithful to that mate, and promote their cause, but if they are insecure in who they are it's never going to change their mind. If the devil starts working in that situation, they are always going to feel threatened. They are always going to feel afraid. They'll want to move you as far away as they can, and they will even try to take you out. Look out for insecure people.

Saul became jealous, fearful, and full of rage toward David. In fact, he was so full of rage that on two occasions he took a spear in his hand and tried to pin David to the wall **(1 Samuel 18:10-11 and 19:9-10)**. The Bible says that the second time that happened, David fled and escaped from Saul's presence. You see, when someone does not like you and the devil gets involved, hidden feelings are bound to come out.

At first, the Bible says that all Saul did was eye David with jealousy. Sometimes, A preacher can look out in the congregation and can tell who is with him/her and who is not because they sit there just eyeing them and waiting for them to say the wrong thing. That's what Saul was doing when it says he was eyeing David. But as time went by and the devil got involved, there was a murderous spirit that came upon Saul. Saul could no longer hide his true feelings.

These two attacks by Saul represented a major transition in David's life; they took David officially out of Saul's kingdom. This was a very important transition because it marked the time when David would no longer be considered a servant of Saul. From here on David still respects Saul as the king and still loves him as a surrogate father, but now he is transitioned from a son to a fugitive. The lines of division had been drawn and Saul's inner feelings were openly revealed. Before this he had hated David, but he was still promoting him. He hated him but still allowed David to marry his daughter. He hated him but David was still fighting his battles. But now it was all out in the open and David would have to leave the palace.

So why would God allow this to happen to a man that He had anointed to be the next king? Why would God let the man after His own heart lose his job, lose his position, lose the loyalty of his wife, lose his connections, and lose his influence? Why would God allow David to be forced out of the palace?

# CHAPTER 1

## *Establishing a New Kingdom*

Thou shalt not make unto thee any graven image, or any likeness of anything that is in heaven above , or in the earth beneath, or that is in the water under the earth: Thou shalt not bow down thyself to them; for I the Lord they God am a jealous God, visiting the  iniquity of the fathers upon the children unto the third and fourth generation of them that hate me. **(Exodus 20:4-5)**

### Dependency on God

The first thing God is doing when He allows us to be run out of the palace is to re-establish our dependency upon Him. One of the things we know about David is the fact that David had a great love for God. But we also understand that God had a great love for David. God called David "a man after God's own heart." The thing that we need to understand is that the God we serve is a jealous God.

The word "jealous" is not the same kind of word that we think of when we are jealous or envious of one another. The word "jealous" here actually means that God is "zealous toward us." He has a passion toward us. He desires that we make Him number one in our lives. When it comes to worship, God has to be worshipped above everything. When it comes to commitment

God has to be number one in our lives. When it comes to loving Him, He has to be number one. When it comes to our dependency, God has to be Number One. Either He is Lord or He'll be nothing at all. He is not going to sit and wait in line. The God that we serve is a jealous God.

It frustrates the heart of God when we compromise our faith and place our dependency upon the arm of flesh. God wants us to be more dependent upon Him than we are upon people. He wants us to be more dependent upon Him than we are upon our jobs. He wants us to be more dependent upon Him than our friends, our girlfriends, and our boyfriends. He wants us to be more dependent upon Him than our husbands or our wives. Many times, when God is trying to get our attention, He will remove some things from our lives and push us out of places where we have become comfortable in order that He might get our attention. God wants our attention!

**It frustrates the heart of God when we compromise our faith and place our dependency upon the arm of flesh.**

When we first met David, he was chasing after the heart of God and totally dependent upon God. He had been rejected by his brothers. He had been rejected by his father and sent out to watch the sheep. While David was out there all by himself, God was developing a relationship that was second to none. It was while he was watching the sheep that David learned to understand his responsibility toward the sheep and how much they were dependent upon him. He placed that in his heart as a symbol of his relationship that he had with his God and wrote, "The Lord is my Shepherd and I have everything that I need" (**see Psalm 23:1**).

While he was out there in the field, David was totally dependent upon his God and God was his everything. While we do need to thank God for all of the wonderful people and friends God has placed in our lives to bless us, deep down in our heart and soul, we still need to remember that God is our everything and we cannot live without Him.

### From the Field to the Palace

When Samuel showed up at the house of Jesse and anointed David to be the next king, the anointing that David received was not for where he was but for where he was going.  As time went by word of David's musical skill on the harp reached King Saul who was tormented by an evil spirit, and he called on David to minister to him. Saul called him out from watching the sheep to dwell in the palace to be his own personal minister in song to drive those spirits away. Then Goliath came! David rose up and smote the giant and his name became a household word throughout all Jerusalem. The Bible says there was a celebratory parade and the women were singing, "Saul has slain his thousands and David his ten thousand" (**1 Samuel 18:7**). David was actually living in King Saul's palace. That word that he had received from God way back when he was overlooked, rejected, and forsaken in his father's house was now being fulfilled. He is living his prophecy.

Just because one receives a prophetic word from God, it does not usher you onto easy street. We tend to think that once we accepted that word that everything was just going to happen instantly. We felt that we were going to have a microwave prophecy with microwavable fulfillment and within moments we were going to pop it in the oven, press one minute, and all of a sudden, everything was going to come to pass. However, we need to understand that when we receive that word from God, that is just the beginning of the process. After that word is received it will most likely be followed by many tests and spiritual exams that will determine if we have learned the lessons that God our Master teacher desires to instill within us. It is not until we have passed them that God will allow us to advance. Until we pass these life exams we will be tested and retested until we are ready to move to the next stage of our destiny.

David had already passed one test, because he stood up to the giant: but in the eyes of God David was not quite ready to walk in the fullness of his prophecy. So, instead of quickly receiving the blessings, God had to take David through some things. He had experienced success, but now he had to experience failure because the true test of a true man of God is how he handles both success and failure. There are some who can serve God as long as He is blessing them and as long as God is opening the windows of heaven and pouring out more blessings than there is room to receive. There are some who can praise and worship God, as long as everything is fine. Indeed, there many who are all right as long as they are tasting success.

On the other hand, there are some who are only faithful to God as long as they are struggling, because they know how to talk to God in the midst of it. As long as there is failure in their lives, they know how to pray, fast and be faithful in service. However, it seems that as soon as God blesses them, they are not praying like they used to pray. They are not fasting like they once fasted. They are not seeking God like they formerly sought after God. While they struggled, and even suffered, they found strength in their struggle; but when success came, the holes in their character was revealed as they discovered that they could not handle their blessings and remain faithful to God.

David, at this point, is beginning to experience a modicum of success. He has now gone from being an unknown to a well-known; from the sheepfold to the palace, and everything was wonderful. David was on the fast track: the king recognized his ability. David was all hooked up, living large and becoming a big baller, as we say in the hood. He was in the palace, and everything appeared to be wonderful, until God would orchestrate yet another transition.

### Transition!

As human beings we are conditioned to routine and repetition and because of that we often find transition uncomfortable and unsettling. I dare say that many of us don't like transition because transition requires the "C" word that we don't like to hear. It requires "Change". We seem to enjoy the comforts of familiarity. We revel in our established tradition and desire that everything to be done as was done in the days of old. However, when God is really about to do something in our lives, He ushers us to and through the uncomfortable and often turbulent waters of *Transition.* David was comfortable in the palace, and I can imagine that the comforts of Kingdom living began to cause him to lose that awareness of His need to be totally dependent upon God. It was time for the wise Master Orchestrator that is our God to push David out of the palace.

It would be here that God would use the jealousy and venom of King Saul to push David toward a difficult transition that would eventually be transformed into yet another step toward his place of destiny. On two different occasions Saul tried to kill David with his spear and eventually David would be forced to flee from the palace in order to save his very life. At that point David had lost everything that was related to palace privileges. He lost his position. He lost his wife. He lost the closeness of his friend, Jonathan. God knew that the rejection that David would experience would not kill David, but he would have been killed if he tried to stay connected to a kingdom that no longer wanted him.

Know therefore that the Lord thy God, He is God, which keepeth covenant and mercy with them that love him and keep his commandments to a thousand generations; and repayeth them that hate him to their face, to destroy them; he will not be lax to him that hateth him, he will repay him to his face. **(Deuteronomy 7:9-10)**

He is the Rock, his work is perfect; for all his ways are judgment. A God of truth and without iniquity, just and right is he. **(Deuteronomy 32:4)**

For the word of the Lord is right, and all his works are done in truth. **(Psalm 33:4)**

I want to remind you that when all of your associations, all of your connections, your job and even your church lets you down, God is a faithful God. He stands in the shadows just waiting for you to call upon Him. He'll stand by you when your husband, wife, boyfriend, or girlfriend walks out on you. He'll stand by you when everyone else forsakes you. You can depend on God when friends walk away. You can depend on God when they scandalize you, criticize you, and ostracize you. He is a dependable God. You can depend on Him when they run you out of the palace and it appears that nobody else wants you.

I've been young and now I am old; but I've never seen the righteous forsaken nor his seed begging bread. **(Psalm 37:25)**

### Forced Into the Hands of God Your Protector

David was forced out of the palace to re-establish his dependency upon God. Saul was still physically on the throne, but he had in reality been rejected years earlier because of his disobedience, his arrogance, and his pride (**1 Samuel 15:26-29**). In order for God to properly establish David and a new Kingdom, He has to have him forced out of the old Kingdom  and disconnected from Saul. God wanted to bless and establish David outside  the  existing  system  and  outside of  the  current establishment.

Even though David operated in excellence, God wanted to show David he did not need Saul. God wanted to reveal to him that his divine favor is better than human connections. God's favor has more influence than money, fame, and people in power. If we make up our minds to stand for God, it doesn't matter who tries to block us, God's favor will bless and establish us without the help of the current system. If we belong to God and desire to walk in His righteousness, the favor of God will be upon us and no weapon formed against us will prosper. (**Isaiah 54:17**). When we walk in the favor of God, God will open doors that no man can shut.

You can even find yourselves in a situation like Joseph where you are unjustly locked in a enemy orchestrated prison, but if the favor of God is upon you God will elevate you even in your lowest state. You may feel like you are at a dead end in your journey but through Gods favor God is about to make a way where there is no way. It may seem like everything in your life is going wrong. It seems like you have been forced out of many places, but the favor of God is still upon you and the hands of the divine protector is still guiding.

David fled and escaped and came to Samuel to Ramah which is in Naioth in Ramah. **(1 Samuel 19:18)**

God was preparing David to establish a new kingdom. The word "Ramah" means "habitation, a dwelling place, a high place." Saul heard about him being there and pursued him causing David to flee to Adullam. The word "adullam" means "justice." David was forced out of the palace to dwell in a high place and then forced to a place of justice. He was run out of the palace to dwell in a high place of justice. David's step down was actually a step up. You don't see it right now but your step down is a step up. They thought that when they walked out on you, they would break your heart and ruin your spirit, but you need to wait on God because your step down is a step up. They thought that when they forced you out of that position that it would result in your destruction, but God will use their actions to re-position you for the next move of God in your life. Indeed, your step down was a step up.

## Time to Establish a New Kingdom

God is about to upgrade you because they pushed you out and thought they were going to kill you, but your step down was a step up. What we have here is a three-step process when a new kingdom is being established.

(1) Being In ···that's the palace.

(2) Being Ousted ···they pushed him out.

(3) Being Blessed···experiencing the favor of God.

God put David out to bring David in. He puts you out to bring you in. That's the way God works. He took Abraham out of Ur of the Chaldees to bring him into a city whose builder and maker was God. He had Joseph kicked out of the family circle to put him in as a commander over all of Egypt. Moses was brought out of the house of Pharaoh and was brought into the office of a prophet. The children of Israel were brought out of Egypt to go into the Promised Land. Shadrach, Meshach, and Abednego were taken out of the fiery furnace to re-establish the worship of Jehovah. Daniel came out of the lion's den to a position of prominence. Matthew got kicked out of the tax collector's office to become a preacher and a representative of God. Andrew and Peter went out of the fishing business to become fishers of men. Paul got put out of the Pharisee's religion and got placed into the office of the Apostle.

Saul's kingdom was characterized by the elite people. God took David out of the old kingdom and established the new kingdom based upon a new principle. He was going to build this new kingdom on misfits and throwaways.

## Cave of Adullam

David therefore departed from there and escaped to the cave of Adullam. So, when his brothers and all his father's house heard it, they went down there to him. And everyone who was in distress, everyone who was in debt, and everyone who was discontent gathered to him. So, he became captain over them.

And there were about four hundred men with him. **(1 Samuel 22:1-2 NKJV)**

David was pushed out of the palace and had to hide in a cave. There, in that cave God was moving behind the scenes to establish a new kingdom. It was not based upon the priorities of the old kingdom. It was based on something new. God wanted to do something new. David became captain of the cavemen, but these men were no ordinary cavemen. There were skilled warriors and most of all they loved David. God connected them with David at a time when he was busted, bruised, and broken. God wanted David to know that there were people who could be trusted. They were not connecting to him because they wanted a promotion because he did not have anything to which to promote them. They were just there because God sent them, they loved David, and they loved David's God.

If you're feeling lonely because you've been pushed out of the palace let me encourage you to hang in there because God is using that event to re-establish your dependence on Him. He's about to build a new kingdom in your life. Get prepared and be ready because you've been pushed out to be brought in and God has a blessing for you!

**Key Points:**
- It frustrates the heart of God when our dependency is upon the arm of flesh.

- God pushes us out of places where we have become too comfortable.
- We are run out of the palace to dwell in a high place of justice.
- God is to be our everything; we cannot live without Him.
- When we are run out of the palace, He is waiting.
- Depend on God when friends walk away.
- Our step down is actually a step up!
- God wants our attention!
- He pushed us out···
- To bring us in!

### Ask Yourself:

1. Is God number one in my life?
2. Do I really totally depend on God or do I have areas in which I place inordinate trust in other sources?
3. Do I have the kind of relationship with God where He is my everything?
4. Can I handle success as well as failure with God as my protector and provider?
5. Am I ready to allow God to push me out so He can bring me in?

### Declare:

"I have been run out of the palace to dwell in a high place of justice. I know that my step down is actually a step up. I will depend on God when friends walk away when they scandalize, criticize, and ostracize me! When they run me out of the palace, I am running straight to Him. I know I am being pushed out so He can bring me in! I am ready for the next phase of the preparation process!"

# SECTION TWO

# FRIENDS

There are those who will trade personal convictions, standards, and even identity in order to be favored by the establishment. They will lose their own self-respect by bowing at the throne of compromise trying to meet the demands of those in power just for the opportunity to be accepted or promoted. Compromising everything they know is right for the hope of upward movement and acceptance in certain circles is both sad and pathetic to see.

## *Without a Price Tag*

Then Saul said unto his servants that stood about him, Hear now, ye Benjamintes; will the son of Jesse give every one of you fields and vineyards, and make you captains of thousands and captains of hundreds. That all of you have conspired against me, and there is none that showeth me that my son hath made a league with the son on Jesse, and there is none of you that is sorry for me or showeth unto me that my son hath stirred up my servant against me, to lie in wait, as at this day? **(1 Samuel 22:7-8)**

Regardless of what area of operation, what organization or profession you may be in, nobody likes a sell-out. There is something disgusting, distasteful, and even putrid about an individual who would trade their personal convictions, standards, and even their identity in order to be favored by an establishment that is unjust and unfair. It is tragic to see people lose the respect of those who admired them as well as to trade their self-respect by bowing at the throne of compromise as they attempt to meet the oppressive demands of those in power. To lose so much just for the opportunity to be accepted or promoted. I'm sure we all agree that this type of behavior is something that is pathetic and extremely sad to observe.

People who engage in this type of behavior seem to lose sight of real truth and can no longer discern the difference between that which is right and that which is wrong. They seem to have decided to compromise everything they know that is virtuous, right, fair, and true just for the hope of upward movement and acceptance in certain circles. What is sad is that after jumping through hoops and making deals with the devil to get ahead, they often find out they have sacrificed way too much along the way. When they get to where they thought they wanted to be, many wonder if it was really worth it. The truth is it isn't how high you go in life that really counts but it's how you got there that makes the difference.

A person can climb the ladder of success rung by rung and still end up being a failure if they have traded things that are eternal for promotion. There are too many who live their lives as though they are for sale and unfortunately, they have sold themselves out. They have even stepped on people on their way to the top. I believe that God is still looking for those in our society who are determined that they will not be bought. People who will stand up for God with a sense of integrity and will not be influenced or bought by the things the world has to offer. People who are determined to do the right thing regardless of the cost.

**It isn't how high you go in life that really counts but it's how you got there.**

Our society seems to be full of people who live with a price tag on them. These people have sold their integrity and even their commitment to God for a price. These people will stand with evil and sell out friendships for the sake of making a few dollars, to fit in with the "in crowd," and to stay connected to people of influence. These are people like Esau, who will trade their spiritual birthright for a mess of political and religious pottage. They are like Judas, who will betray those close to them for thirty pieces of silver. They will even send you to the Cross if it means getting ahead and being promoted. "Everyone has a price" seems to be the underlying mind-set of our age.

As a man who was raised in the church and who loves the church it saddens me that there are many who have suffered the pain of abandonment and rejection in the church in exchange for church politics and public appearance. For them the church is no longer their place of safety but now has become a place where they feel like they can no longer enter and find peace and serenity. Because of betrayal by friends who secretly came with a price tag on them the house of healing has now become the house of pain. May God provide healing and refuge for all who are reading and have become a victim of wounds that have taken place in the house of their friends.

We are living in a society in which the value systems of our people have become so corrupt that people will practically do anything in order to move forward even if it involves violating their own morals and personal convictions. I still believe that God is looking for some people who will stand for what is right and refuse to be cheapened by being bought. God is looking for people without a price tag.

God will never leave us without people in our lives who really have a heart for us. God will always have somebody near us who loves us enough to be willing to go the extra mile and look out for us regardless of what it may cost them. That fact is evident in the life of David. He is forced out of the palace and is in hiding as a fugitive, moving from cave to cave and from camp-to-camp fleeing from King Saul. God sends him an army of misfits that are willing to go the distance with him even though King Saul has vowed to kill him and everyone who is connected to him. David must now transition and be both a servant and a leader to keep those willing to follow him safe.

In the meantime, King Saul is also looking for those who will be willing to prove their loyalty to him by positioning themselves against David. When he wants to find out where David is hiding, he holds a meeting with his officials and the men of Benjamin, under a tamarisk tree, on a hill in Gilboa with a spear in his hand (1 Samuel 22:6).

I need to stop here and make a parenthetical statement; always be careful when someone wants to meet with you, and they still have their spear in their hand. What that means is that this individual is there to try to intimidate you into doing what they want you to do and will even go as far as to take you out if you are not careful. One of the interesting things we learn about General Colin Powell in his book, "Leadership Secrets of Colin Powell" is he had a habit of coming from behind his desk in order to sit with individuals so that he could meet with them on even terms. That's the kind of friend that you need to have in your life; somebody who is willing to meet you on even ground.

Saul is trying to shake down his men in order to get information from them concerning the whereabouts of David so he can capture and kill him. He is using intimidation to get his men to follow him and do what he wants them to do. He has resorted to leading by intimidation. That is why God had to get David away from the old leadership style and place him in a new environment so he could learn how to lead in a manner in which God wanted His kingdom to operate. David was being prepared to lead and establish this new kingdom.

As David's story develops, there are actually three main characters with whom Saul deals. One of these characters is a sell-out by the name of Doeg, and the other two are both priests, Abimelech and Abiathar who were "Friends Without A Price Tag."

# CHAPTER 2

## *People Who Have Intrinsic Values*

I have preferred to be true to myself even at the hazard of incurring the ridicule of others rather than to be false and incur my own abhorrence. ~ **Fredrick Douglas**

Friends without a price tag have intrinsic values. The word "intrinsic" actually means "belonging to the real nature of a thing; it is that which is not dependent upon external circumstances; it is those things which are essential, inherited, which is located within." They are those invisible things that you cannot put your hands on but are worth more than all of the money, all of the popularity, and all of the things that this world has to offer. These are inner qualities such as character, dignity, love, gentleness, integrity, and self-respect. People who have intrinsic values understand the value of these inner qualities and refuse to trade them for anything.

Frederick Douglas said, "I have preferred to be true to myself even at the hazard of incurring the ridicule of others rather than to be false and incur my own abhorrence." In other words, there are some things about me that are on the inside that I refuse to change, that I refuse to let go of, and that I refuse to trade for anything. Those of you who are searching for friends and relationships make sure you don't base your decisions upon external things. External things, as wonderful as they are, have the ability to change and fade in the long run.

## What's on the Inside?

One of the reasons a lot of marriages are not working today is because people are going into them based on all the wrong criteria. We want to marry that man because they are cute, but cute doesn't pay the bills. We want to be with her because she is pretty or has a good job or has money. However, if marriage is going to work it has to be based on more that external things. It has to be based on more than biceps and triceps, bank accounts and prestige or hips, lips, and fingertips. Money can dry up, and regardless of how good they might look; eventually Father Time and gravity are going to catch up with everybody. Those lips, hips, and fingertips will become lisp, sips, and drips. That junk in her trunk, as they say in the hood, is eventually going to become sag in her bag. His pecks will turn into wrecks and those muscles will eventually become mush. We must learn that we've got to make decisions based upon more than external things. We've got to make sure that there are some intrinsic values that we love about that individual. We need to make sure that they have some character, integrity, and intelligence.

One of the problems today is we are looking in the mirror that is above our dresser drawers and on our bathrooms walls more than we are looking in the mirror that is the Word of God. We are reading the Bible without allowing the Bible to read us. We're building up the external things instead of those things that we need to have on the inside. We've got to allow God to work on us within and help us to develop intrinsic values. A real friendship is not based on what we have or what we can do for them. Real friends are not with us based on how we look because real friendship is based on something they see on the inside of us. We can easily judge the character of a person by how they treat those who can do nothing for them. That's the kind of friend we need to have in our life. We need those who are going to be there whether we have money in the bank or we are broke, busted, or disgusted. Those are the kind of friends that have intrinsic values.

**We can easily judge the character of a person by how they treat those who can do nothing for them.**

In a meeting under a tree on the hill, Saul begins to talk to his men and appeal to the external things he can do for them. Will the son of Jesse give you fields and vineyards? Will he make all of you commanders of thousands and commanders of hundreds? Is that why you have conspired against me? No one tells me when my son makes a covenant with the son of Jesse. Not one of you is concerned about me or tells me that my son has incited my servant to lie in wait for me as he does today. What has David done for you materially? What does he have to offer you? Like Janet Jackson would say, "What has David done for you lately?"

Saul is so far away from God that he does not have anything else to offer them except material things. He has backslidden and has lost his anointing as a man of God. Now the only things he can offer them are things that are external. He is also trying to intimidate them and buy them into being loyal. Friendship that is bought will never last or will never be paid in full. Sooner or later there is always a higher bidder.

All the devil has to offer are material things and fear. He wants to offer things that appeal to the flesh. He instills fear that we might not fit in with everybody else or will never get anywhere in life. God is looking for somebody that's made-up their mind to stand for God and say to the devil, "Regardless of what you have to offer me, my mind is made up. There is no price tag on me! For God I'll live and for God I'll die! "

## Doeg the Edomite

Then answered Doeg, the Edomite, which was set over the servants of Saul, and said, I saw the son of Jesse coming to Nob, to Ahimelech the son Ahitub. Ahimelech inquired of the Lord for him and he also gave him provisions and the sword of Goliath, the Philistine. **(1 Samuel 22:9)**

Unfortunately, there was somebody on the scene who did not have those intrinsic values. His name was Doeg, the Edomite. After Saul gave his speech, Doeg decided that he was going to stand up and say something. Doeg the Edomite decided to sell David out along with Ahimelech in order to get favor with King Saul. The name "Doeg" means "fearful, anxious, timid, and sorrowful," and let me add "wimp, coward, and one who when I grew up was called a tattletale." He ran right into the boss to get favor from man.

There are some so-called friends that will sell us out just for the opportunity to go forward. There are some co-workers who will try to ruin our careers so they can go forward. There are some people who will attempt to put your light out thinking that somehow it will cause their own to shine brighter. There are some people that will smile in our face and stab us in the back in order to get promoted. We've got to look out for Doeg because the fact of the matter is, Doeg is a coward. He is a wimp. He is somebody who looks at the truth and what is right but makes a decision that is inherently selfish. Doeg reports Ahimelech and his family to King Saul and puts all of the priesthood of that area in danger.

When one has a *price tag* on them, they don't care about anybody but themselves. It's all about how "me, myself, and I." How I can get ahead, how I can get promoted, and what can I get for me. When there are no intrinsic values with a selfish person like this, they don't care who gets hurt or who dies. The only important thing is me, myself, and I.

A person like this can climb the mountain, cut people off, trample on individuals, and appear blessed. But the truth is that the same people they trampled over on their way up they will see them again on their way down because God is keeping score. He's still watching everything. They might think they are slicker than Willie, but God's got their name and number. They may receive a temporary promotion, but there will come a day when they will have to pay the price for all of their deeds.

Doeg thought that he was getting ahead, but he was making a terrible mistake. He should have let God promote and bless him. He didn't have to resort to dirty tricks and sell his integrity. God is calling you and I to be a friend without a price tag. We can't afford to be numbered among those like Doeg. There are some things that are worth more than popularity, more than money, and worth more than promotion. That's what Jesus told His disciples, "Take heed and beware of covetousness for a man's life consisted not in the abundance of things which he possesseth" **(Luke 12:15)**. Then in Mark 8:36-37 He said, "What shall it profit a man if he shall gain the whole world and lose his soul? What shall a man give in exchange for his soul?" Paul says, "For the kingdom of God is not meat and drink; but righteousness and peace, and joy in the Holy Ghost" **(Romans 14:17)**.

Shirley Chisholm has said, "I'm a fighter. Nobody has ever bought me or bossed me!" In other words, there are some things in me that are not for sale!

**Key Points:**
- A person's character is shown by how they treat those who can do nothing for them.
- It isn't how high we go in life that really counts but how we get there.
- We must have some things within us that are not for sale.

- God is looking for people without a price tag.
- Friendship bought will not stay bought.
- There is always a higher bidder.
- We must not lose our soul.
- We live for God!
- Him only!

## Ask Yourself:

1. Am I for sale?
2. Do I have standards I will not compromise?
3. Do I have intrinsic values?
4. Am I a friend that cannot be bought?
5. Will I be true to myself even at the hazard of incurring the ridicule of others rather than to be false and incur my own abhorrence?

## Declare:

"I've still got holiness and I've still got Jesus. He's all that I need. I didn't get the promotion, but I still have my Jesus. I lost the job, but I still have Jesus. I lost my popularity, but I still have my Jesus. I lost a few friends, but I've still got my Jesus. I have a feeling that everything is going to be alright. I don't play patty cake with the devil. There are some things in me that are not for sale!"

# CHAPTER 3

## *People Who Understand Real Friendship*

Greater love has no one than this, that he lay down his life for his friends. **(John 15:13 NIV)**

Observing the way that people react and interact with each other has convinced me that there are not many people in society who really understand the real meaning of friendship. If somebody claims to be a friend but won't speaks to us anymore after a disagreement or break off a friendship over minor issues, never really was a friend in the first place. A real friend will work it out because they have love and history with us. They see our friendship as something that is worthwhile, something they can work through with us, and will work to preserve the friendship. Understand that friendship is not blind loyalty where they support everything we do even if we are wrong. Friendship is not losing our identity to someone else and having no opinion of our own. A real friend will help us to love God more. A real friend will celebrate when we get blessed, go the extra mile for us, warn us of impending danger or disaster, and watch our back at all times

The biblical word for "friendship" is the Greek word *philos* which involves the idea of loving as well as being loved. Another Greek word is *heteros* which means "a comrade, companion or a partner." Then there is a Greek phrase *hoi para autou* which means "one who is beside you." So a real friend is one who loves, is a comrade, and walks beside us through thick and thin, in good times and in bad times. They walk beside us when we're up and when we're down. A friend is someone who walks in when the whole world walks out. That's what a real friend is all about.

## Ahimelech

Then the king sent to call Ahimelech the priest, the son of Ahitub, and all his father's house, the priests that were in Nob: and they came all of them to the king. And Saul said, Hear now, thou son of Ahitub. And he answered, Here I am, my lord.  And Saul said unto him, why have ye conspired against me, thou and the son of Jesse, in that thou hast given him bread, and a sword, and hast enquired of God for him, that he should rise against me, to lie in wait, as at this day? **(1 Samuel 22:11-13)**

The test of friendship is not when we are on the mountains of life. The test of real friendship is when we find ourselves walking in dark places. Ahimelech the Priest is about to show us that he is David's real friend. The king had said his speech. Doeg had spoken up and squealed on David. Now Ahimelech finds himself in a bad situation.

Then Ahimelech answered the king, and said, And who is so faithful among all thy servants as David, which is the king's son in law, and goeth at thy bidding, and is honourable in thine house? Did I then begin to enquire of God for him? be it far from me: let not the king impute anything unto his servant, nor to all the house of my father: for thy servant knew nothing of all this, less or more. **(1 Samuel 22:14-15)**

Saul is so blind and so far away from God that he accuses David who loves him of doing the very thing of which he is himself engaged in. Ahimelech didn't just stand there and listen to Saul's false accusations concerning his friend. "If you want to know the truth," Ahimelech said to King Saul, "This is not the first time that I have prayed for David, seeking for God to provide for David." Ahimelech had already made up his mind that he was not going to back down even if it cost him his life. This was a man who understood the real meaning of friendship. A real friend will defend us when we are not there to defend ourselves. That's how we know when we have a real friend. They will stand up for us whether we are present or not.

There are some folks who'll act like they're with us until our backs are turned. We've got some so-called friends who'll allow others to walk in and speak bad about us. They are open to hear gossip, but a real friend will stand up for us and tell the truth. That's the kind of friend that we need. We need somebody that's going to bless and defend us even when we're not there. We need to rid ourselves of folks who do not know whether they are for us or against us. If we have friends that are wavering back and forth and are double minded, we can't waste our time with them.

**False friends will roll out the carpet for you one day and pull it out from under you the next day.**

As a matter of fact, the name "Ahimelech" means "the brother of the king." The word "brother" there is the word *adelphus* or *adelphia* which denotes a brother or near kinsman. In the plural it means "a community band or identity or origin of life." Philadelphia means "the city of brotherly love." The opposite of that word is "pseudo delphi" and that word means "false friends." One of the problems we often run into is that we have too many false friends who look at us and smile, but they really don't mean us any good. They'll shake hands while secretly on the inside they wish that we would choke and die and go away. False friends are those who will roll out the carpet for you one day and pull it out from under you the next day. Ahimelech refused to allow anyone to falsely accuse David and he took a stand even if it cost him his life. He was a real brother!

I thank God for "Friends Without a Price Tag" because they'll stand up for us when it's uncomfortable. Saul decides that he is going to have David's friend taken out and ordered the guards to kill the priests, but the guards refused (1 Samuel 22:17). They understood that if they touched the priests, it would bring a curse upon their own lives. False friends will encourage us to do things that will bring a curse on our life. We need to stay away from people who are always trying to nudge us to do the wrong things.

Stay away from those who are trying to encourage you to do what's wrong, to walk in rebellion, and do other things that are against what you know is right in the eyes of God. You're really walking in danger trying to be loyal to some so-called friends. Stay away from a friend that's encouraging to you to walk your way straight into a devil's hell. Stay away from people who try to buy you with things so they can hold you hostage for the rest of your life. Stay away from people who are going to try to bring a curse upon you.

These guards made up their minds that even though they were in the camp and were Saul's guards, they were not going to touch God's anointed and bring a curse upon themselves. Stay away from people who try to encourage you to do the wrong thing.

### The Edomite

A maskil of David.

When Doeg the Edomite had gone to Saul and told him:

**"David has gone to the house of Ahimelek."**

[1] Why do you boast of evil, you mighty hero?

Why do you boast all day long,

you who are a disgrace in the eyes of God?

[2] You who practice deceit,

your tongue plots destruction.

it is like a sharpened razor.

[3] You love evil rather than good,

falsehood rather than speaking the truth.

[4] You love every harmful word,

you deceitful tongue!

[5] Surely God will bring you down to everlasting ruin:

He will snatch you up and pluck you from your tent;

he will uproot you from the land of the living.

[6] The righteous will see and fear;

they will laugh at you, saying,

[7] "Here now is the man

who did not make God his stronghold

but trusted in his great wealth

and grew strong by destroying others!"

[8] But I am like an olive tree

flourishing in the house of God;

I trust in God's unfailing love

for ever and ever.

[9] For what you have done I will always praise you

in the presence of your faithful people.

And I will hope in your name,

for your name is good. **(Psalm 52:1-9 NIV)**

The fact that it says Doeg is an Edomite is significant because these people operated by different laws. They were governed by the works of the flesh. He decided that he would do what Saul told him to do even though he knew it was wrong The Bible says that he rose up and killed Ahimelech, and his whole family **(1 Samuel 22:18-19)**. Ahimelech died, but his son Abiathar took off and was able to escape with his life. He met up with David and told him all that had happened and what Saul and Doeg had done **(1 Samuel 22:20-21)**.

So David said to Abiathar, "I knew that day, when Doeg the Edomite was there, that he would surely tell Saul. I have caused the death of all the persons of your father's house. Stay with me;

do not fear. For he who seeks my life seeks your life, but with me you shall be safe." **(1 Samuel 22:22-23 NKJV)**

Abiathar means "father of plenty." When you decide to choose right you may not get hooked up, you may not get into the "in crowd," but God will see to it you will be a father of plenty. He'll open up the windows of heaven and pour out blessings that there will not be room enough to receive. Abiathar was later appointed high priest by King David. Abiathar was David's friend and stayed with David during the critical days of Absalom's revolt.

Abimelech and Abiathar were "Friends Without a Price Tag." God is looking for people who are without a price tag! He is looking for people like Moses who would rather suffer affliction with the people of God than to enjoy the pleasures of sin for a season. He is looking for people like Joseph who will not sleep with Potiphar's wife even if it means being thrown into jail. He searches for people like Shadrach, Meshach, and Abednego who will say, "We know that our God is able to deliver us out of the fiery furnace but even if He doesn't, we still won't bow down." God seeks men like Daniel who said, "Go ahead and throw me into the lion's den, but I'm going to pray and seek the face of God." And He seeks women like Esther who said, "If I perish let me perish, but I'm going to see the king and do what I can to save my people."

### What a Friend We Have in Jesus!

I thank God for earthly friends who do not have a price tag. Most of all, I thank God for the One who stood up for me even before I knew Him over two thousand years ago. The devil could not buy Him. The Pharisees and the Sadducees could not buy Him. The people could not purchase Him. Even pain could not deter Him from paying that ultimate price for me! He could have called ten thousand angels to rescue Him, but He hung there because He was my Friend. I thank God for a friend who went the extra mile.

### Key Points:

- False friends roll out a carpet one day; pull it out from under us the next.
- A true friend blesses and defends us even when we're not there.
- A true friend knows whether they are for us or against us.
- A true friend walks in as the whole world walks out.
- A true friend watches our backs no matter what!
- A true friend won't bend or compromise!
- A true friend celebrates our successes!
- A true friend goes the extra mile!
- A true friend can't be bought!
- A true friend stands true!
- Jesus is my friend!

## Ask Yourself:

1. Do I have so-called friends who don't know whether they are for me or against me?
2. Do I hang out with those who roll out the carpet one day and pull it out from under me the next?
3. Am I the kind of friend who will defend my friends even when they aren't there?
4. Do they do the same for me?
5. Do I celebrate when my friends get blessed, go the extra mile for them, warn them when they are on the wrong path, and watch their backs?
6. Do they do the same for me?
7. Do I have those among my friends that God is showing me I need to say good-bye to?
8. Do I have the courage to obey?

## Declare:

I will not be bought! I know that my God is able to deliver me out of the fiery furnace, but even if He doesn't, I still won't bow down and compromise my stand for Him.

# SECTION THREE

# SAUL

Never take the trauma of rejection so hard that you end up running to just anyone for acceptance. There are some places you can run to that are full of ravenous wolves and sharks that smell blood and will take advantage of you in your vulnerable state.

## *My Surrogate Father Gone Bad*

And Saul took him that day and would let him go no more unto his father's house. **(1 Samuel 18:2)**

In Book One, I shared with you the wisdom of God in managing our affairs in such a way that for every father like Jesse who overlooks us, God provides a Samuel who is there to lay hands on us and affirm us. It is a wonderful thing and a blessing to know that God loves us enough to have someone there to help to make up for the pain and agony that we experience when we are rejected and overlooked by those who are supposed to embrace us and make us feel loved and protected. God is so concerned with our development that he sends someone to serve as a surrogate or a substitute and to be the catalyst to aid us on the road to destiny.

It is, however, vital that we never reach a point in our experience that we become so needy and desperate to be picked up and accepted that we are not careful about whom it is that picks us up. Don't ever become so wounded that you will try anything or go just about anywhere to find your healing. Never take the trauma of rejection so hard that you end up running to anyone for acceptance. There are some places that you can run to that are full of ravenous wolves and sharks that smell blood. They will take advantage of you in your vulnerable state. There are places that are like snake-pits where there are snake-like people who will use you as a pawn to fulfill their lustful desires for power, control, money, success, and even sex.

**Don't ever become so wounded that you will try anything or go anywhere to find your healing.**

All too familiar is the story of that desperate person, seeking for affirmation who runs blindly into the arms of false healers. They were looking for Mr. or Miss Right but who they ended up with was ever so wrong. They were so hurt that they ended up in the clutches of Mr. Could Have Been Right or Miss Should Have Been Right or Almost Right. Maybe they ended up with a Sugar Daddy or a Sugar Mama who left them with nothing but a sour taste in their mouth.

They ran to Rev. Wonderful who was really Rev. Fill My Pockets with your money. They went to church and met Pleasant Pete who was nothing but a Pentecostal Pimp. Instead of being healed through someone they picked, they found they were just moving from one system of abuse to another, from one abusive relationship to another, and from one distorted father or mother image to an unhealthy connection. They found they had moved from the place of pain and emptiness into the grip of a surrogate who had gone bad.

What is a surrogate? *The Webster's New World Dictionary* defines it as a "deputy or substitute; a person of some authority who replaces a father or a mother in one's feelings; one who is put in another person's place." Now, for those of us who have been in the Church, we fully understand the concept of the surrogate relationship. As a matter of fact, one of the practices that is commonplace in the history of the Church is that of referring to those in the church as brother, sister or mother. It is actually a practice that goes back to the days of slavery. During that time many people experienced displacement and separation as families were being torn apart by that evil and ungodly institution. It was commonplace for those of the household of faith to step in and serve as a surrogate to someone whose parents had been torn from them and moved to a different plantation. We understand that the idea of a surrogate is a powerful thing.

**God indeed specializes in the use of surrogates.**

A close look at the Scriptures reveals to us that God specializes in surrogates and substitutes. When Adam fell, an animal was slain as a substitute covering for Adam's sin. The priests of the Old Testament sacrificed lambs to atone or substitute as the price of man's transgressions. It was a ram that God provided for Abraham to serve as a substitute to be slain in the place of his son. Jesus Christ is called the" Second Man, Adam." He was a surrogate or a substitute to die for our sins. When Jesus went back to heaven, He told His disciples He was going to go to His Father and pray that He will send us another comforter; someone just like Jesus to serve as a surrogate to teach us and guide us. God indeed specializes in the use of surrogates.

Many times, in order to strengthen, mature, and develop us, God will use certain individuals to be substitutes in our lives that we might be blessed and developed into what God has called us to be. However, anyone who has knowledge of the devil understands that for everything that is godly, real, and positive the devil will try to create a counterfeit. We need to be continually cautious and recognize the counterfeits! For every real mentor there is a fake mentor hoping to get to us first. For every healthy substitute there are unhealthy ones. For every God-sent friend there is a devil-sent false friend. For every God-ordained spiritual father and mother there are false fathers and mothers. For every real apostle and minister there are false apostles and ministers. For every real surrogate there are surrogates who have gone bad.

It always amazes me how God can raise great people out of broken situations. The fact is that God does not need perfect circumstances or surroundings to shape the person through whom He desires to use to do great things. Such was the case for David, the man whom God chose to be His king over Israel. We understand that David's life was no walk in the park. He had to endure the pain of being rejected by his father and hated by his brothers. Also, in the critical relationship of the father to his son, David was overlooked by his very own father. It was here in this vital relationship that an area of vulnerability developed that would serve to haunt and affect David for the rest of his life.

It was in this state of vulnerability that the devil launched his attack. He would use Saul as one of his tools to try to hinder and block David from his seat of assignment. That is how the devil works. He tries to find an area of vulnerability in each and every one of our lives. Then he tries to convince us to participate in filling that area in the wrong way. Whether we want to admit it or not, all of us have an area of vulnerability. All of us have a place of lack in our lives. I don't care how successful you are. I don't care what kind of family lineage you come from; somewhere in the course of your life there is an area of emptiness. The question is how are you going to fill that area of emptiness?

That is where the enemy attacks because he wants to get us to fill it in the wrong way. For David, this improper filling came in the form of a man by the name of Saul. Saul is one of the most tragic figures in Scripture. He has the distinction and the honor of being Israel's first King, but he served in such ineffectiveness and failure that he failed to make the roster of the great men listed in the Hebrews 11 "Hall of Faith." Saul faced the temptation that everyone who has gone from nothing to something faces; the temptation to forget the place from which God has brought them. We have a lot of people in the church that have somehow forgotten where God has brought them from and what God has done for them. Saul was a man who had all of the opportunity in the world. He was chosen even though he did not have the qualifications. Then because of his arrogance, his disobedience, and pride, God had to take the kingdom out of his hands.

And Saul said unto Samuel, I have sinned: for I have transgressed the commandment of the Lord, and thy words: because I feared the people, and obeyed their voice. Now, therefore, I pray thee, pardon my sin, and turn again with me, that I may worship the Lord. And Samuel said unto Saul, I will not return with thee: for thou hast rejected the Word of the Lord, and the Lord hath rejected thee from being king over Israel. And as Samuel turned about to go away, he laid hold upon the skirt of his mantel, and rent it. And Samuel said unto him, The Lord hath rent the kingdom of Israel from you this day, and hath given it to a neighbor of thine, that is better than thou. And also, the Strength of Israel will not lie nor repent: for he is not a man, that he should repent. **(1 Samuel 15:24-29)**

Because of his disobedience, Saul arrived before the prophet and finally admitted he had sinned and disobeyed instructions and the Lord's commandments. Then he offered an excuse saying he was afraid of the people and did what they demanded. At this point Saul asks the prophet to forgive his sins and go with him to worship the Lord, but Saul's request was rejected because Saul had chosen to reject God's word. Not only was he not forgiven by Samuel, but Saul was also told that God was going to take the kingship away from him and give it to another.

After his rejection, an evil spirit came and began to torment him. He began to seek for somebody to come and play skillfully on the harp and soothe his troubled spirit. That person would be David. Saul took a rejected David and moved him from the sheepfold into the palace and basically became a type of surrogate father for David. The Scripture tells us that Saul chose him to be his cupbearer and that Saul loved him. What we will find out is that because of the emptiness in David's life, he also grew to love Saul and actually ended up loving him as a father.

The problem was that as David began to move toward his destiny, Saul crossed that thin line that lies between love and hate. Instead of loving David, rejoicing, and celebrating with David as he moved toward his destiny, Saul fixed in his mind that he was going to do everything that he could do to keep David from ever getting on track. Saul, like most false surrogates, came into David's life during a time when David was hurting and vulnerable after being rejected by his father and his brothers.

What can we do to avoid becoming attached to the wrong type of surrogate? How do we avoid connecting with someone who will hinder us as opposed someone who will help us? How do we make sure the person we are in relationship with is not going to hold us back instead of releasing us into our destiny? How do we avoid having that surrogate damage and abuse us as opposed to being an instrument of healing? We can study how David moved out from under this surrogate gone bad and was able to continue his journey to establish a new kingdom.

# CHAPTER 4

## *Be Discerning When Searching*

There are a few things you and I can look for and do if we are going to avoid falling into the hands of a surrogate who has gone bad. The first thing is we need to use **Discernment.** The gift that is most needed in the Church in the times in which we are living is the **Gift of Discernment.** In our day of itching ears, pop theology, and everyone is walking around like "parking lot prophets" claiming they hear from God, we need to have a spirit of discernment. The word "discernment" actually means to "search, examine closely, inquire carefully, and to conduct a judicial search."

There are basically two types of discernment that we need in these last days. The first is the spirit of discernment concerning the discerning of spirits. This has to basically take place on the spur of the moment. "Beloved, believe not every spirit, but try the spirits whether they are of God; because many false prophets are gone out into the world" **(1 John 4:1)**. This scripture says there will come times when you and I will be confronted by certain spirits that will try to cower, hide, and disguise themselves as being from God. We must be at a point in our relationship with God in which we are instantly able to discern between that which is God and that which is not God.

One day there was a woman who came into the sanctuary where I was pastoring. As the service started, she stood up, began to spin around in circles as if she was prophesying. Immediately God spoke to my spirit and let me know that she was not of God. I signaled to the ushers to take her out of the sanctuary. We found out later that this same woman who had been in the church was walking down the road with a knife talking about what she wanted to do to me and our local Bishop. You have to be in a place where you can recognize whether somebody is prophesying, walking in a gift that is from God or from the devil. Don't you believe everything somebody tells you.

There is another type of discernment that is a little more complex because it is the **discerning of people and their motives.** You have to come to a point in your experience with God where you allow Him to speak to you concerning the people that are around you. There are some folks who will smile at you, say certain things, and want to get close to you, but deep down in their spirit they want nothing but death and destruction for you.

When Jesus was here on earth, He was confronted by many individuals. The Bible often says that Jesus discerned or knew what was in them. Therefore, when they came to Him claiming to be one thing and they were something else, Jesus had such a connection to His Father that He knew what was in them. "When they had seen the miracles that Jesus did, they said, 'This is of a truth that prophet that should come into the world.' When Jesus therefore perceived that they would come and take him by force, to make him a king, he departed again unto a mountain himself alone" **(John 6:14-15).**

But there were certain of the scribes sitting there, and reasoning in their hearts, Why doth this man thus speak blasphemies? Who can forgive sins but God only? And, immediately when Jesus perceived in his spirit that they so reasoned within themselves, he said unto them, why reason ye these things in your hearts? **(Mark 2:6-8).**

Notice it says immediately Jesus knew in His spirit what they were thinking. There were times when Jesus came into direct conflict with individuals who were seated in the crowd among His followers. They thought that they could trick Him, but there was something deep down in His spirit that would let Him know who was for Him and who was against Him; who was sincere or who was phony; who was real and who was disingenuous. He had a spirit of discernment.

## Do a Spiritual Background Check

Do not be in a hurry in the laying on of hands [giving the sanction of the church too hastily in reinstating expelled offenders or in ordination in questionable cases], nor share or participate in another man's sins; keep yourself pure. **(1 Timothy 5:22 AMP)**

Paul told Timothy not to be in a hurry to lay hands on people. The "laying on of hands" was a symbol of acceptance and of authorization. Paul was telling Timothy not to choose people hastily. Do not ordain them right away. He needed to take some time to find out what they are all about. Paul was telling Timothy that before he lets somebody into his life, do a background check. Before you allow them to take you under their wing, before you allow them to be your surrogate, do a background check. Before you allow them to be your mentor, your prayer partner, your covenant buddy, spiritual father, spiritual mother, armor bearer or whatever you need, do a background check. Check out what their spirit is all about. Check out their motive and see what it is all about. Get on your knees and ask God about them.

Look for some consistency in their life. Look at the relationships that they have had with those they have mentored in the past. Look to see if they are a model that you can see yourself replicating. Check out their record. Check to see if they are balanced because you don't want someone who is so heavenly minded that they are no earthly good. Make sure you find somebody that's got their feet on the ground and their head in the heavens. If they are talking about taking you under their wing, find out what kind of wing they are trying to put you under. Are they trying to put you under a chicken wing or a turkey wing or do they have eagles' wings? You have to do a background check to find the answers to these questions.

**Find somebody that has their feet on the ground and their head in the heavens.**

There is too much craziness going on in the Church for you to just come under anybody without doing a background check.

Nowadays, we have homosexuals infiltrating the church. We have child-molesting deacons infiltrating the church. We have serial stalkers and sexual predators sitting in our churches. Before you let anybody take you under their wing and be a surrogate in your life, you need to do a background check. Before you marry that man, you need to do a background check. Before you hook up in any relationship, you need to do a background check. Don't lay hands on them until you check them out. That person trying to rush you down to the altar to marry them might be trying to hide something. You need to take some time and get to know them. Don't let your flesh push you into something where you are going to be trapped and end up miserable. That person might be trying to hold you back or trying to possess you for one reason or another. Make sure you have enough patience and discernment to do a background check.

David found himself in an unfortunate situation. He did not have a choice in being picked up by Saul. The rule of the day simply was that if the king called you, you had to go. We know that an evil spirit came and began to torment Saul. He looked for somebody who had skill on the harp to come and play for that spirit to release him **(1 Samuel 16:14-23)**. When David showed up and did this, Saul loved him and decided to take him from his father's house.

When David was promoted from the sheepfold to the king's palace, it all looked good. Be careful though, if it sounds too good to be true, most of the time it is too good to be true. God helps us to discern.

### Key Points:

- If it's too good to be true, it probably is too good to be true!
- Don't ever become so wounded that you'll try anything.
- God indeed specializes in the use of surrogates.
- We need to look out for the counterfeit!
- Do a background check beforehand.
- God helps us to discern.
- Seek discernment!
- Be discerning!

### Ask Yourself:

1. Have I done a background check on this person who wants to be my surrogate?
2. Have I taken the time to get to know something about this person?
3. Am I sure he or she is not a counterfeit sent to move me off track?
4. Is what is happening too good to be true?
5. Does this person have their feet on the ground and their head in the heavens?
6. Are they someone I can see myself replicating?

### Declare:

I will not be in a hurry to accept a surrogate in my life. I will have the patience to do a background check and learn something about this person first. I will pray and ask the Lord for discernment concerning this person. I will not move forward until I believe God has given me the go ahead for this relationship.

76

# CHAPTER 5

## *Never Choose Out of Desperation*

Desperation is a powerful force that drives people to do things that they would not normally do in ordinary circumstances. There are a lot of men and women in Correctional facilities around the world that are not there necessarily because they are bad people. There are a lot of people that are there because they found themselves in desperate situations. Interestingly, a definition of "desperation" is "the state of being desperate; recklessness resulting from despair; driven to or resulting from the loss of hope." It also means "having a great desire or need." Desperation is a powerful force! It actually is a force that can bring about both bad as well as good results.

On the positive side there are people who won't move unless they get desperate. Desperation will move a person to action. It will make you act when you don't want to act. One of the most interesting stories in the Bible is the story of the "Prodigal Son." This young man ran away from his father and spent all that he had. When he found himself in the pig pen, he had an unfulfilled need. He was about to eat pig's food because he was desperate. That desperate need brought the prodigal son to his senses. It made him think about his choices and it spurred him into positive action **(Luke 15:11-20)**.

On the other hand, there is a negative effect. Whenever someone is in a position of desperation and has lost hope, it seems to limit their options. Desperation almost forces one to make unwise choices.

## *Desperation Can Move a Person to Action.*

### Emotional and Spiritual Desperation

Emotional and spiritual desperation can allow the devil to step in and use people to bring confusion into our lives. It can lead us into places where unhealthy soul ties develop. Too often in the midst of pain, we try to medicate our pain by being with another person. However, just because God has someone there for us in a time of crisis that does not mean it is meant to be lifetime and permanent relationship. Be careful and steer away from asking help from people who are always rehearsing what they did for others. It is a sign that they think that once they help someone that person is forever indebted to them and will often attempt to use that debt as a means of manipulating and controlling others.

A real minister understands that he or she is just a bridge and an instrument to be used by God. We can step into somebody's life to bless them and our involvement with them can be permanent or temporary. As real ministers, we recognize that we can be there for somebody just for a season. Some of us have gotten ourselves into relationships where we have said, "You saved my life, I owe you. I'll be your servant for the rest of my life." Somebody helped us during a time of crisis and we have become a slave to them because we think we owe them!

I am not talking about being unthankful. However, we need to look out for the kind of person who thinks because we got desperate and came to them, now we owe them. They will even try to take credit for our success. Real ministers don't respond like that because we realize that we are just instruments to help bring about healing and provision on behalf of our God.

**A word of advice: Never make major decisions in a season of frustration and pain.**

Some of us got in a bad situation because we became desperate. That is one of the ways that Saul played on David. David was on the rebound. He was already rejected and hurting. Saul offered him an opportunity and had David feeling like he was finally somewhere where he could be accepted. The Bible says David grew to love Saul as a father. Saul liked David very much and David became one of Saul's armor bearers. Then Saul sent word to Jesse asking him to let David join his staff because David pleased him. Whenever the tormenting spirit from God troubled Saul, David would play his harp and the tormenting spirit would go. David is picked from the sheepfold and placed in the palace. Now he is there but the problem is that he has gone from being rejected to being used.

Pain on top of pain! Rejection on top of rejection! Hurt on top of hurt! Confusion on top of confusion! Out of the frying pan and into the fire. Some of us got involved with people when we were on the rebound. We hooked up with that so-called spiritual person because we were on the rebound and now we are sleeping with the enemy. Now we are attached to the person who actually wants to destroy or even kill us.

A word of advice: Never make major decisions in a season of frustration and pain. Spend some time with God and allow Him to do some healing before you make a lifetime decision based on temporary circumstances.

You can't make decisions when everything is cloudy, and you are in pain and desperate. You need to wait until the clouds clear. You need to wait until you find some healing before you make another decision before you hook up with someone else. Don't make a decision out of desperation. Wait until the rain stops falling! You need to wait until the clouds clear and you can see the picture more clearly. Wait until your healing begins to set in. Sometimes in the midst of desperate situations you don't need to move. You need to stand still and chill!

## Stand Still and See the Salvation of the Lord

Moses answered the people, "Do not be afraid. Standstill, and see the salvation of the Lord, which He will accomplish for you today. For the Egyptians whom you see today, you shall see again no more. The LORD will fight for you, and you shall hold your peace." **(Exodus 14:13-14 NKJV)**

The children of Israel were marching up to the Red Sea. The army of Pharaoh was coming up behind them. They were in a desperate situation. They panicked. They started complaining and murmuring, but Moses says: "Stop worrying. Stop getting desperate. God is still with us. Stand still and see the salvation of the Lord. Stand still!"

Stop running to and fro, from person to person, and from relationship to relationship. Stop going from one broken heart experience to another broken heart experience. Get alone with God and allow Him to heal your broken heart. Find yourself in the secret place of the Most High God and let Him bring healing and deliverance in your life. If you'll stand still, He'll part the Red Sea for you. If you'll stand still, He'll make a way out of no way. If you'll stand still, He'll bring healing in your life. If you stand still He will bring somebody into your life who is going to be a blessing and not a curse. Stand still!

**Stand still and God will bring somebody into your life who is going to be a blessing and not a curse.**

Some of us need to understand that you don't have to be with somebody to be somebody. You don't have to be in a club, a sorority, fraternity or popular to be somebody. You are somebody because God has made you somebody. Even though the tears may be rolling down your face, you are somebody. Even though you may have to walk by yourself, you are somebody. You might think that you are by yourself, but you are not. You might think that you are alone, but you are not alone.

David said, "Yea, though I walk through the valley of the shadow of death, I will fear no evil: for thou art with me; they rod and thy staff they comfort me" **(Psalm 23:4)**. You can say the very same thing!

### Key Points:

- Stand still and God will bring one into your life who is a blessing and not a curse.
- Never make any major decision during a season of frustration and pain.
- Desperation may try to force one to make unwise choices.
- Never make any major decision out of desperation.
- Desperation can move a person to action.
- Stand still; see the salvation of God.
- Wait and see what God will do.
- God will make a way!
- Don't lose hope!

### Ask Yourself:

1. Am I in a position of desperation?
2. Am I in danger of losing hope?
3. Have I allowed desperation to limit my options and try to force me into making unwise choices?

**Declare:**

"I am not going to make a decision when everything is cloudy and I am in pain and desperate. I will wait until the rain stops and the clouds clear. I will wait until I find some healing from God before I make another decision, and before I hook up with someone else. I will no long make my decisions out of desperation."

# CHAPTER 6

## *Avoid the Green-Eyed Monster - Jealousy*

Set me as a seal upon thine heart, as a seal upon thine arm for love is strong as death; jealousy is cruel as the grave: the coals thereof are coals of fire, which hath a most vehement flame. **(Song of Solomon 8:6)**

Jealousy is a deadly force. The word "jealousy" in the Hebrew means "to be zealous for." That's the good side of it. God is a jealous God which means that He has a zeal for you. He wants to be number one in your life. There is another meaning to that word that is evil. It means to look upon someone, see their excellence, and then want to make war upon the good in them. This kind of jealousy is because that person does not see that same excellence within themselves. That war is made with the intent of troubling and diminishing that good in the other person. Watch out for jealous people!

If ever I sense that someone close to me has a jealous spirit, I have learned to do one of two things. I am going to give them a chance by letting them understand how I got to this place. Some people see the glory, but they do not know the hell and the high water that person had to go through to get blessed like you are being blessed. Many of those who are envious and jealous wouldn't trade shoes with them for half a second if they knew what they had to go through to get there. So first I'll let them try to understand the story behind the glory. If that doesn't work, I'll just simply stay away from them.

Jealous people get crazy and will try just about anything to war against you and take you out. Jealousy is always a sign of insecurity and manifests in possessiveness. Rodney Dangerfield said, "My wife is so jealous that she looked at my calendar and asked me who May was?" Look out for jealous, insecure, possessive people.

Some of you got into relationships with insecure and possessive people. At first it seemed cute when you saw them two minutes ago, walked down the road, and they called you on your cell phone. "They are just so in love with me," you thought. You got home and they called you on your home phone. "This is just so wonderful, so beautiful." Then they began calling you throughout the night making sure that you were alright. What they were really doing was making sure that you were still at home. Their calls and possessiveness will quickly escalate into jealousy, rage, a spirit of control and even violence. Jealous people will do strange things for jealousy is as cruel as the grave.

## King Saul's Jealousy

Saul has slain his thousands and David his ten thousand (1 Samuel 18:7)

Saul became David's surrogate father and as long as David was there as a servant, everything was fine. Whatever Saul asked David to do, David did it successfully. Saul even promoted David to be his cupbearer which showed the level of trust that he had for the former shepherd boy because the cupbearer was responsible for making sure the Kings food was not poisoned. But after David killed Goliath, the women came out from all the towns along the way and celebrated. First, they were cheering for King Saul and they sang and danced for joy. But all of a sudden Saul became angry and said, "What is this? They credit David with ten thousand and me with only thousands. Next, they will be making him their king" **(1 Samuel 18:8 TLB)**. From that time Saul (in the King James Version) says that Saul began "to eye David" **(1 Samuel 18:9)**. The New International Version of the Bible says, "Saul kept a jealous eye on David."

All of a sudden, the person who loved David while he was the servant became jealous. The same person that loved him when he was broke, busted, and disgusted now is angry at David's success. The same person that promoted David is afraid of him because David has achieved a higher level of success than Saul had achieved.

Look out for jealous people. Don't attach yourself to anybody who doesn't want to see you go farther than they have gone. Make sure that if you submit to someone to be your surrogate, they have a vision in their heart for you and will take pleasure in seeing you do things that they themselves have never done. Make sure that you don't covenant with someone who is going to push you down instead of lifting you up. Jealous people will put roadblocks in your way and try to kill your dreams and vision. Make sure you get connected with somebody that has a vision for you to succeed even to a higher level than they have ever reached.

### Elijah and Elisha

And it came to pass, when they were gone over, that Elijah said unto Elisha, ask what I shall do for thee, before I be taken away from thee. And Elisha said, I pray thee, let a double portion of thy spirit be upon me. And he said, Thou hast asked a hard thing: nevertheless, if thou see me when I am taken from thee, it shall be unto thee; but if not, it shall not be so. **(2 Kings 2:10-11)**

We need to have a surrogate father like Elijah was to Elisha. Elisha had followed Elijah everywhere. When Elijah asked Elisha what he wanted, Elisha said, "I want a double portion of your spirit. I want to do twice as much as you did." Elijah had the heart of God and did not mind seeing Elisha go farther than he had gone. Elijah performed sixteen miracles, but Elisha performed thirty-two **(2 Kings 2:1-12)**. That is the kind of surrogate that you want to be around. You need somebody who doesn't mind seeing you mount up with wings as eagles. You need a surrogate who doesn't mind seeing you soar to farther heights than they have gone.

Jesus Christ was that kind of surrogate. "Verily, verily, I say unto you, He that believeth on me, the work that I do shall he do also; and greater works shall he do; because I go unto my Father" **(John 14:12)**.

I do not believe that anyone should allow another to be their surrogate that does not want to see them go farther than they did. Beware, because in your time of need and desperation, they will seek you out. If you have already tied up with them and now they have proven to be a surrogate gone bad, it is time to cut the cord.

Stand fast, therefore, in the liberty wherewith Christ hath made you free, and be not entangled again with the yoke of bondage. **(Galatians 5:1)**

## Key Points:

- A surrogate should have a vision in their heart for our success.
- Jealous people will put up roadblocks to try and block us.
- Jealousy is a deadly force and as cruel as the grave.
- Jealousy is always a sign of their insecurity.
- Jealous people tend to be possessive.
- Watch out for jealous people!
- It is time to cut the cord!
- Jesus made you free!
- Be not entangled!
- Be free!

## Ask Yourself:

1. *Do I have some soul ties that are affecting my destiny?*
2. *Am I tied to an individual that is insecure, jealous, and possessive?*

3. *Is this soul tie keeping me from doing what God wants me to do?*

4. *Is God showing me it is time to cut the cord with this person?*

**Declare:**

"I am cutting every unhealthy soul tie. I'm cutting the cord. I praise God for my liberty right now. In the name of Jesus, I shall be free of this possessive and restrictive relationship. I know that whom the Son sets free is free indeed. I am free!"

# SECTION FOUR

# ENEMIES

We must realize that oftentimes those God sends to be instruments of our perfection do not come to us wrapped in the bows and ribbons of positive relationships. Sometimes they come in the jagged edge boxes that contain our enemies and our foes.

## *To Bring Out My Best*

Saul called back, "Is it really you my son, David?" Then he began to cry and he said, "You are a better man than me, David, for I have repaid your good for evil. **(1 Samuel 24:16 NLT)**

Oftentimes when we consider those, we believe are anointed to bring out our best our minds immediately are brought to the ones who stand by our side through thick and thin, weep with us when we are down, rejoice with us during our seasons of accomplishments and victory, and encourage us with words of affirmation and comfort. We must, however, realize that sometimes those anointed to be instruments of our perfection do not come wrapped in the bows and ribbons of positive relationships. Sometimes they come in the jagged edged boxes that contain our enemies. There are those that try to come against us and, in one way or another, attempt to assassinate our character and our reputation.

What we often fail to understand is that God will use even our enemies for a specific purpose. He is so wise and so awesome in His dealings with us that He balances our lives with healthy doses of anointed friendships but also allows us to have certain enemies that He uses as refining tools to test our character and to reveal the depths of our Christian virtues. What we fail to realize is that the real test is not how we handle our friends but how we respond to our enemies.

Anybody can function when the whole congregation is on their side. Anyone can be successful when everyone shares their vision and is in complete co-operation with them. Everyone can love their best friend and their favorite people. But what separates the men from the boys, separates the women from the girls, and the saints from the "ain'ts" is how we deal with those that have been planted around us who are against us. It's how we function in that organization when it is sprinkled with people who simply want to see us fail. It's when there are terrorist cells hidden in the camp that are trying to plant explosives in an effort blow up all of our plans and our vision. It's whether or not we respond with love toward the people who are in oppositions to us and are waiting for the day we fail; people that actually have party supplies sitting on standby waiting for our downfall so that they can celebrate it. How do we deal with our enemies?

**I thank God for my friends who pray for me, but I also thank God for my enemies that make me pray.**

God is trying to develop real leaders of integrity and power. He works through and develops us by allowing our enemies to come into our lives to bring out the best that is in us. I thank God for my friends who pray for me, but I also thank God for my enemies that make me pray. If you have some enemies, you are to be congratulated because it is a sign that you have stood for something. No man has ever amounted to much without arousing jealousies and creating enemies. So having enemies is not altogether a bad thing for it is evidence that we are trying to accomplish something good. If we were just sitting back and minding our business and not trying to do anything, everybody will like us and everybody will be on our side. When we have the audacity and the gall to actually rise up and be everything that God has called us to be, we can guarantee that there will be those who will try to take us out.

There is really no way we can examine the life of David without continually re-visiting the relationship he had with King Saul. This relationship was indeed a complex one. While David had a consistent and steadfast love for Saul, it seems as though Saul could not quite figure out how he felt about this young surrogate son and soon to be successor. Because the Spirit of God had departed from him and he was afflicted with an evil spirit, Saul seemed to be unstable in his relationship with David.

One moment he loved David, and the next minute he was filled with hatred toward him and was trying to take his life. Believe it or not, Saul's behavior toward David actually is indicative of some of the behavior pattern that our enemies have toward you and me. If the truth be known, our enemies often really admire us deep down inside. The like what we're all about, but instead of sharing our joy they become jealous because of their own insecurities. They begin to feel that they'll never quite measure up and never quite get the things that we have attained. Instead of blessing us, they behave in a childish manner and look for an opportunity to take us out.

It is because of this very principle that we find David fleeing for his life. As Saul and his team of specialized assassins are pursuing David, we find him surrounded by a group of misfits who are highly skilled warriors that have said in their hearts they are going to protect David until he reaches the throne that God had promised him. However, we are about to see that God is going to cause a reversal of fortune to take place in the life of David. Saul had just returned from pursuing the Philistines when he is told that David and his men were in the desert in Engedi. He gathered three thousand warriors and sends them to search for David among the rocks and the wild goats (1 Samuel 24:1-2). Little does Saul know that while he is searching for David, everything is about to be reversed. The hunter is about to become the hunted; the trapper is about to be trapped.

"That he came to the sheep's pen. Along the way a cave was there and Saul went in to relieve himself and David and his men were far back in the cave" **(1 Samuel 24:3 NIV)**. Little did Saul know that he had actually walked into the very same cave where David and his warriors were hiding. David creeps up on Saul and has Saul right where he wants him. How David responds to his enemy will reveal his real character. We will see from this opportunity how God uses our enemies to bring out the best in us.

# CHAPTER 7

## *The Tests – Discernment and Biblical Principles*

When we go to any kind of school, we take evaluation tests to discern how well we have learned the lessons we will need to be released to go to work in our chosen field. David had certain tests while he was a shepherd boy living in his father's house. Then he had a different set of tests when he graduated to the next level of his training when he served in the palace under King Saul. Now in the wilderness, David is about to experience an even higher level of testing. God will use David's enemy to test David's level of discernment and his commitment to God's principles.

### The Discernment Test

God uses our enemies to test our discernment. One of the things we are constantly reminded of is that the greatest gift needed in godly leadership today is not the Gift of Prophecy and not the Gift of Healing although those are important. What we really need is the Gift of Discernment. That is, we need the ability to make wise decisions, not only in trying spirits but in discerning people and situations. The reason this is so needed is that life can get complicated makes decision making extremely difficult. Charles Carlson said, "Life isn't like a book. Life isn't logical or sensible or orderly. Life is a mess most of the time and theology must be lived in the midst of that mess."

Real discernment is needed when the picture is not quite clear. When there seems to be grey areas, we need the wisdom of God to determine what decision needs to be made in that particular situation. It is real difficult when a situation arises when what appears to be the right thing to do is actually the wrong thing to do.

David actually faced that type of situation, hiding in the same cave where King Saul chose to relieve himself. David and his men were far back in the cave when the men said to David, "This is the day the Lord spoke of when He said to you, 'I will give your enemy into your hands for  you to deal as you wish'" **(1 Samuel 24:4)**. Saul had been seeking David's life. Now David seemed to have Saul right where he wanted him. Everything looked like a divine set-up. It looked like God had put Saul in David's hands. David's men sure thought so and logic sure points in that direction. Good battle strategy would indicate clearly what the next move should be.

**Just because the Lord gave you a promise it does not mean that He is going to violate His own principles to get it done.**

However, here is where godly discernment must kick in. Just because the Lord gave you a promise it does not mean that He is going to violate His own principles to get it done. The problem is there are people who hear the voice of God but fail to understand the principles of God. They do not use wisdom and discernment and think the end justifies the means. God is not just concerned about why you get what you get, but how you get what you get. It is not who you are with but how you got with who you are with. Even though we know that God wants to bless us to be a blessing, that does not mean we are to pray to God to give us somebody else's home or somebody else's property. God want us to have the perfect spouse, but we are not to ask God to give us somebody else's spouse. There are some people who are praying for God to bring death to someone so they can have what that person has. People who pray that way have lost all sense of discernment.

We need to understand that we need a discerning spirit because if we are not careful the devil will try to tell us it's a God-thing. Just because it looks good, doesn't mean it is God. Everything that glitters is not gold. Everything that looks right does not mean that it is right.  We've got to have some discernment, or the devil will fool us and get us to move in the wrong way.

As the heavens are higher than the earth so are my ways higher than your ways, and my thoughts than your thoughts. **(Isaiah 55:9)**

Trust in the Lord with all of thine heart and lean not to thine own understanding. Acknowledge him and he shall direct thy path. **(Proverbs 3:5-7)**

One of the things that David understood was that there are ways that might seem right to us that are wrong in the eyes of God. There are situations that might look like God is moving in them, but it is far away from what God has in mind. David had the spirit of discernment and would not accept this situation because it violated the Laws of God.

Afterward, David was conscience-stricken for having cut off a corner of his robe. He said to his men, "The LORD forbid that I should do such a thing to my master, the LORD's anointed, or lay my hand on him; for he is the anointed of the LORD." With these words David sharply rebuked his men and did not allow them to attack Saul. And Saul left the cave and went his way. **(1 Samuel 24:5-7 NIV)**

## The Commitment to Biblical Principles Test

God also uses our enemies to perfect our commitment to biblical principles. Our problem today is not the fact that people are not getting enough teaching and preaching. Our real problem is whether or not we are going to be obedient to the Word that we already know. Most of us can quote it, but is it part of our life? We can watch it on TV, but can we live it? Many of us know from experience that there are situations that can arise in our lives that will test what we really believe about biblical principles, especially when it comes to this whole issue of revenge. It's hard to do what God says to do when you have somebody like Saul who is trying to assassinate you and bring you down. When the opportunity comes and it looks like God has given them to you on a silver platter, you need to look deep in your heart and analyze your response.

When Saul walked into that cave all by himself, it looked like a Divine Set-up. David's men thought, "This has got to be God! If God didn't want it to happen this way, He would never have set it up this way!" David knew he could take Saul out, but he also knows what God's Word said concerning touching His anointed. David decided that he was not going to murder Saul. He still does not totally do the right thing either. He crept up on Saul and cut off the corner of Saul's robe. Even though he did not kill Saul, it was not right for him to do what he did.

David became convicted about what he did to King Saul. Sometimes God will set up a situation to test us to see if we're still going to go past emotion and be obedient to His Word. God will use a Saul situation to create for us what I call those "surprise moments." They are moments when we're surprised at how we handled it. We look at what we did and can't believe that was the way we responded. What we do next determines whether or not we pass the commitment to biblical principles test.

David could have killed Saul, but David had a heart after God and was determined to be obedient to the Word of God. The Bible says that after David cut off his robe, he was conscience-stricken. David had a heart that wanted to be obedient to God's Word. Even though he was in a situation where he could have gotten even, he lived by a principle that was larger than him.

## Doers of the Word

Be ye doers of the Word and not hearers only deceiving yourselves. **(James 1:22)**

Anybody can be obedient when it's convenient. Anybody can be obedient when everything looks right. David is in a situation where he could get out of the cave, but he makes up his mind that he's going to be obedient to the Word of God. The Bible says that David turned to his men and said, "Men, I know I could have taken him out. I know I could have killed him. I cut off his robe instead, but I want you to know that was not right either. He's still God's anointed and even though it looks like I could have gotten even and could have been right, I can't go against the Word of God. I know what my enemies would've done to me. I know what my flesh and emotions wanted to do and I know what you as my friends wanted me to do, but I can't go against the Word of God."

That is what the decision-making process is really all about. It's not about how we feel or what we want to do, it's about what God's Word has to say about it. We can't live our lives based on emotion. We can't live our lives based on how we personally feel about it or even what the situation looks like. We've got to come to a point where we can say, "God, if Your Word tells me to do it, that's what I'm going to do. If Your Word tells me not to do it, then I won't." In fact, Jesus told us exactly how to handle our enemies and follow biblical principles.

"I say unto you, love your enemies. Bless them that curse you. Pray for them which despitefully use you and persecute you that you may be children of your father which is in heaven. For He maketh His son to rise on the evil and on the good. He sendeth rain on the just and the unjust. He said if you love them which love you what reward do you have? Even the sinners and the publicans do that." **(Matthew 5:46-48)**

"Bless them that curse you. Pray for them that despitefully use you." **(Luke 6:28)**

"Bless them which persecute you. Bless and curse not. Rejoice with them that do rejoice and weep with them that weep. Be of the same mind one toward another. Mind not high things, condescend to men of low estate. Recompense to no man evil for evil. Provide things honest in the sight of all men. And if it be possible as much as lieth in you, live peaceably with all men. Dearly beloved, avenge not yourself. Avenge not yourselves. Neither give place unto wrath for vengeance is mine," saith the Lord. **(Romans 12:14-19)**

God's Word make us excited and can cause us to feel good when we are in the House of God. It feels good when we are worshipping together. But the real question is, when we are out there in our daily lives are we willing to be obedient to what God's Word has to say? Are we really willing to bless those that curse us and pray for those that despitefully use us? God is looking for some people who are going to be obedient even when it does not make any sense.

**Key Points:**

- Discernment is needed or the devil will get us to move in the wrong way.
- The Lord will not violate His own principles to fulfill a promise.
- Real discernment is needed when the picture is not quite clear.
- Just because something looks good doesn't mean it is God.
- Everything that looks right does not mean that it is right.
- Anybody can be obedient when it's convenient.
- Life isn't logical or sensible or orderly.
- Everything that glitters is not gold.
- Be a doer of God's Word!
- Life isn't like a book!
- Life is confusing!
- Obey God!

**Ask Yourself:**

1. How do I function in a place sprinkled with people who want to see me fail?
2. How do I respond?
3. What do I do when things get so complicated that what appears to be the right thing to do is actually the wrong thing to do?
4. Can I love my enemies and do what God says to do?

5.  When I go about my daily life am I a doer of the Word?

6.  Am I willing to be obedient to what God's Word has to say?

7.  Am I willing to bless those that curse me and pray for those that despitefully use me?

### Declare:

"I thank God for my friends who pray for me, but I also thank God for my enemies that make me pray. I don't have time to just sit still and let life pass me. God has called me to do something and the fact that my enemies are against me is an indication that I'm on my way somewhere. I thank God for using them to bring out the best in me. God, if Your Word tells me to do it, that's what I'm going to do. If Your Word tells me not to do it, then I won't. I will love my enemies and do what Your Word tells me to do!"

# CHAPTER 8

## *God Uses Our Enemies to Increase Our Influence*

Behave yourselves wisely [living prudently and with discretion] in your relations with those of the outside world (the non-Christians), making the very most of the time and seizing (buying up) the opportunity. Let your speech at all times be gracious (pleasant and winsome), seasoned [as it were] with salt, [so that you may never be at a loss] to know how you ought to answer anyone [who puts a question to you]. **(Colossians 4:5-6 AMP)**

Whether we realize it or not there are people who are watching how we respond to our friends and to our enemies. What is at stake is not just our reputation but our influence and our leadership! People are going to decide whether or not they're going to follow us based on how we handle our enemies. People want to know if we are going to follow the Word of God not just when it's convenient but when it's difficult. They want to see if we're going to maintain our faithfulness or stoop to the level of our enemies. If we are going to increase our leadership influence, we cannot stoop and fight on the same level as our enemies. If we do then we will lose the respect of those who are watching us.

One of the reasons Christians have lost the respect of those who are on our jobs and in our families is because we have lowered ourselves and are fighting at the same level as those enemies that are around us. If we are going to have real influence, we've got to live in a way that is above those whom God has placed to follow us. A business that has to resort to attacking a competitor's product instead of trying to convince potential customers the value of purchasing theirs is stooping to the level of the world. They hit me below the belt so I'll hit them below the belt sounds fair, but is it proving to those what are watching me that I'm faithful to the biblical principles I claim to follow?

David realized that the men he was called to lead were watching how he was going to respond to them as well as to those that were against him. There are some people who may even urge us to take revenge. Then as soon they see us cross the line, they will turn to somebody else and say, "I thought that person really loved God. They disappointed me in the way they handled that particular situation." That's why we've got to stand by God's Word and be able to discern the situation always realizing that our influence is at stake.

But then his conscience began bothering him. "I shouldn't have done it," he said to his men. "It is a serious sin to attack God's chosen king in any way." These words of David persuaded his men not to kill Saul. **(1 Samuel 24:5-7 TLB)**

The word "persuaded" means "to tear them apart." When David spoke with that level of conviction upon his life, his words literally tore his men apart. They wanted to go in one direction but David rebuked them and said we don't do things like that. We don't operate on the same level as our enemies do. David's words and his life had influence.

If you're going to have influence you've got to equal life and lip. You cannot say it's about what I say and not what I do. If you're really going to have influence, you've got to walk in obedience to God before those that are around you watching you.

Because David was obedient to the Word, his men decided to be obedient to him and did not touch Saul. Because of the way David handled this situation with his enemy, his influence actually grew and affected Saul.

After Saul had left the cave and gone on his way, David came out and shouted after him, "My lord the king!" And when Saul looked around, David bowed low before him. Then he shouted to Saul, "Why do you listen to the people who say I am trying to harm you? This very day you have seen it isn't true. For the Lord placed you at my mercy back there in the cave, and some of my men told me to kill you, but I spared you. For I said, 'I will never harm him—he is the Lord's chosen king.' See what I have in my hand? It is the hem of your robe! I cut it off, but I didn't kill you! Doesn't this convince you that I am not trying to harm you and that I have not sinned against you, even though you have been hunting for my life? "The Lord will decide between us. Perhaps he will kill you for what you are trying to do to me, but I will never harm you. As that old proverb says, 'Wicked is as wicked does,' but despite your wickedness, I'll not touch you. And who is the king of Israel trying to catch, anyway? Should he spend his time chasing one who is as worthless as a dead dog or a flea? May the Lord judge as to which of us is right and punish whichever one of us is guilty. He is my lawyer and defender, and he will rescue me from your power!" **(1 Samuel 24:8-15 TLB)**

The Bible says that when Saul saw David and heard these words, he began to weep and he called him son and told David, "You are a better man than I am."

And he said to David, "You are a better man than I am for you have repaid good for evil.   Yes, you have been wonderfully kind to me today, for when the Lord delivered me into your hand, you didn't kill me. Who else in all the world would let his enemy get away when he had him in his power? May the Lord reward you well for the kindness you have shown me today. And now I realize that you are surely going to be king, and Israel shall be yours to rule. Oh, swear to me by the Lord that when that happens you will not kill my family and destroy my line of descendants! **(1 Samuel 24:17-21 TLB)**

Even David's enemy Saul realized what David had done by not responding in the wrong manner. God allowed this opportunity in David's life to bring out the best in him and the same time influence those who were watching him. Now even his enemy Saul saw this man David was worthy to be the king.

### I Thank God for My Enemies

I know it might sound strange and even crazy to some, but I thank God for my enemies. I thank God for the people that came against me and tried to stop me because I've found out that God used them to bring out my best. I thank God for my enemies for without them I would never have known what God had placed inside of me. I would never have known that if God be for me who can be against me. I even thank God for racism because I found out that there's a door that no man could open and there is a door that no man could shut.

I thank God that there were those who hated me because I learned that I could still love my enemies. If there had not been those who rejected and overlooked me, I would never be able to testify, "If it had not been for the Lord on my side where would I be?" I found out that I'm accepted by God, and that I have a friend that sticks closer than a brother. I thank God for my enemies for without enemies I would never have found out how anointed I am, how much power I've got, and how much glory God has placed on the inside of me.

The Songwriter Andrae' Crouch said in his classic song "Through it All". "I thank God for the Mountains; I thank Him for the Valleys and I thank Him for every storm He's brought me through. For if I never had a problem, I wouldn't know that God could solve them. I'd never know what faith in His word can do." God used my enemies to bring out the best in me, to take me to the next level, and who caused me to  pray consistently. God brought me out of where He did not want me to be and anointed me to be a leader in His kingdom because of those enemies.

## Key Points:

- We can't stoop down and fight at the same level as our enemies.
- We can't say, "Do what I say and not what I do."
- We've got to walk in obedience to God.
- We've got to stand by God's Word.
- We've got to equal life and lip.
- Our influence is at stake.
- We're being watched.
- God is faithful!
- God is love!

## Ask Yourself:

1. Am I thankful for the mountain, the valley, and every storm?
2. Can I see that if I'd never had a problem, I would not have discovered what faith in God and His Word can do?
3. Can I see that God used my enemies to bring out the best in me?
4. Can I see God's purpose in bringing me out of where He did not want me to be?
5. Can I now thank God for my enemies?

## Declare:

"I thank You God for the mountain, the valley, and every storm. I know that if I'd never had a problem, I would not have discovered what faith in You and Your Word can do. I thank You

God for using my enemies to bring out the best in me. I want to continue to move to the next level. Take me to where You want me to be."

# SECTION FIVE

# ABIGAIL

What are the driving forces, motivations, reasons, and underlying needs that cause certain people to not only be attracted to each other but also to develop relationships that eventually turn into soul ties?

## *Hooked Up to a Fool*

One of the many questions that continue to baffle those of us who are involved in relationship counseling and development. Is the question of what motivates people to enter into and develop relationships that possess the potential to result in unhealthy soul ties? What are the driving forces and underlying needs that cause certain people to not only be attracted to one another but to cultivate such relationships? How did Conservative Carl end up with Carefree Carla? How did Diligent Debra who always had a job end up with Lazy Bill who never worked and never will? How did Straight–laced Sally get together with Wild Wayne? How did Classy Claude get together with Foolish Freda? How did that happen?

I am well aware that they say that opposites attract, but I found out that after they attract, they often attack because they find that they do not have anything in common beyond physical attraction. They have not developed the kind of relationship that is based on intangible and godly things that will help to grow both people into the kind of person that God wants them both to be. It is definitely not a waste of time and energy to get to know about the person inside, so we do not end up getting hooked up to a fool. We need to go slow because anybody can pretend to be something that they are not for a short time. Eventually the real person that is hiding behind that mask along with their hidden agendas will come creeping out to show their ugly heads. If we will give it some time, we avoid finding out later on down the road that we've hooked up to a fool.

## David, Nabal, and Abigail

And there was a man in Maon, whose possessions were in Carmel; and the man was very great, and he had three thousand sheep, and a thousand goats: and he was shearing his sheep in Carmel. Now the name of the man was Nabal; and the name of his wife Abigail: and she was a woman of good understanding, and of a beautiful countenance: but the man was churlish and evil in his doings; and he was of the house of Caleb. **(1 Samuel 25:2-3)**

As we continue our journey into the many persons involved in the life of Israel's greatest king, we are reminded that even the greatest king in Israel could not be at his best by surrounding himself with only "The King's Men." There had to be some women involved to help to bring out the best in him. Here we are introduced to a fine, intelligent woman by the name of Abigail. The story here in 1 Samuel 25 is one of passion, danger, irony, and intrigue. As we open this story, David has already killed Goliath. He has received his anointing as the next king of Israel and has taken to living in the wilderness to avoid the jealousy of King Saul whose heart was set on murdering him.

Samuel had just died, and David has moved to the wilderness of Paran hiding from Saul's troops. He is hiding in the mountainous terrain that was too difficult for a regular army to survive in for very long. David's band of men had grown from the original four hundred that met him in the cave of Adullam to over six hundred men. This group that had originally consisted of rag-tag, broke, malcontents, and misfits had now grown into a group of disciplined, sharp, and seasoned warriors living on the edge of trouble.

They were abiding in a land that was far away from governmental influence or an official law enforcement agency. They were basically out in the middle of nowhere. Because of this, David and his men had become the self-appointed peacemakers and lawmakers of the region. Their services were needed as well as appreciated. They would protect the farmers and the sheep herders from thieves and wild beasts. The custom of the land in which they were living was people would offer them blessings in exchange for their service. To refuse to give that kind of blessing to these men was as tantamount as refusing to tip a waiter or waitress who has provided a good service. In other words, it was extremely insulting.

Nabal and Abigail are an example of those opposite type of couples that I spoke about earlier. Nabal was a very wealthy and successful businessman, but he lacked good sense and a good attitude. As a matter of fact, his very name "Nabal" actually means "a fool." Proverbs describes a fool as somebody who is rude, ignorant, dishonest, belligerent, obstinate, and stupid. This was probably not the name his parents gave him, but because of his behavior the people in the neighborhood recognized that he was foolish, so they just began to call him "Nabal."

His wife Abigail was just the opposite of him. As a matter of fact, her name means "My Father's Joy." She was said to be intelligent, ingenious, and industrious as well as very beautiful. How did Abigail find herself attached and hooked-up to such a foolish and terrible man? She was actually the victim of a bad decision that was made by her father. During those times all of the marriages were arranged. A father would choose someone for his daughter he felt was the right type of mate for her. In his case, Nabal must have been able to pull the wools over Abigail's father's eyes perhaps using his wealth and his influence.

David sent men to greet Nabal who had just had a great influx of wealth, partly due to the protection that David and his troops had provided for him. The Bible says that David's men came and suggested to Nabal to give them a gift after they had extended to him the protection and the service in order for him to raise the kind of healthy and robust sheep that he had raised. One would think that Nabal would have been grateful, but Nabal begins to live up to his name. Instead of giving David what he was worthy of receiving, Nabal starts to cut the fool. The Bible says that David's men arrived and gave Nabal the message in David's name. Nabal answered David's men in **1 Samuel 25:10-11**, "Who is this, David? Who is this son of Jesse? Many servants are breaking away from their masters these days. Why should I take my bread and water and the meat that I have slaughtered with my shearers and give it to men, coming from God knows where."

Nabal was belligerent and insulting by calling David a nobody who had no business approaching a rich man. Then on top of that he accused David of committing treason because he was no longer with Saul. When David's men brought that message back, David became angry and decided that Nabal would pay for his foolish attitude and actions with his life. Nabal's foolish mouth had gotten him into trouble. Now David and his troops were on their way to his estate.

A servant came to Abigail and told her that David and his men were on their way. Abigail sprang into action doing three important things to save her home, her servants, and her foolish husband.

One of the servants told Abigail, Nabal's wife, David sent messengers from the wilderness to give our master his greetings, but he hurled insults at them. Yet these men were very good to us. They did not mistreat us, and the whole time we were out in the fields near them nothing was missing. Night and day they were a wall around us the whole time we were herding our sheep near them. Now think it over and see what you can do, because disaster is hanging over our master and his whole household. He is such a wicked man that no one can talk to him.  **(1 Samuel 25:14-17 NIV)**

# CHAPTER 9

# GOOD GIFT, GOOD ATTITUDE, AND GOOD JUDGMENT

Abigail acted quickly. She took two hundred loaves of bread, two skins of wine, five dressed sheep, five seahs of roasted grain, a hundred cakes of raisins and two hundred cakes of pressed figs and loaded them on donkeys. Then she told her servants, took two hundred will follow you. Her servants took two hundred loaves of bread. **(1 Samuel 25:18-19 NIV)**

### Give God Our Best Gift

The first thing we need to do is give God our best gift. In Eastern culture gifts possessed great meaning and power. The word "gift" actually meant a tribute given to an overlord. So, it was the custom of that day that one would never go before a great man without bringing a gift. Abigail understood the power of a gift and quickly prepared a tribute to David and his men that she believed would bring peace. She decided that she was going to get the best gift she could give and bring it to David and his men. Abigail understood the principle that there is a gift that can be presented to the king in such a way that it can actually divert disaster.

When we bring a gift of praise to our Heavenly Father, it can break up the plan of the enemy. God has placed a gift within each one of us and when we bring it before Him as our King, it can be the very key to unlock our deliverance.

Abigail prepared her gift and as David and his troops were heading to bring disaster and destruction to her home, she stands between David, Nabal, and disaster with her gift.

As she came riding her donkey into a mountain ravine, there were David and his men descending toward her, and she met them. David had just said, "It's been useless—all my watching over this fellow's property in the wilderness so that nothing of his was missing. He has paid me back evil for good. **(1 Samuel 25:20-21 NIV)**

Not only did Abigail understand the concept of a gift, but she also understood the attitude of gift giving. She was the wife of a very wealthy man. Notice, however, that she is riding on a donkey. Wealthy people did not ride on donkeys. Notice also what she did as David approached her.

When Abigail saw David, she quickly got off her donkey and bowed down before David with her face to the ground. **(1 Samuel 25:23 NIV)**

Abigail came from a wealthy family and now came before a man who was not yet the king, but she recognized something in him, and she brought her gift to him in the right attitude. She understood that there is no real success without giving the king her best. If we desire more deliverance, we need to give God our best worship. If we want more blessings, than we need to give God our best gift. There's a gift that we can bring to our King that will literally cause the wrath of God to be turned into favor especially when one brings it out of the context of a negative situation, like Abigail has done. Abigail is married to a fool, but she still has a gift to bring to the king.

## Good Attitude - Intercede to the King

*She fell at his feet and said:* "Pardon your servant, my lord, and let me speak to you; hear what your servant has to say. (1 Samuel 25:24 NIV)

Abigail's attitude was one of intercession to the king on behalf of her husband Even though she was hooked up to a fool, she was willing to intercede before the king for the lives of all those subject to and effected by the foolish actions of that fool! To intercede primarily means to meet with, converse with, make a petition to, and especially to plead with someone either for or against others. In other words, somebody approaches the throne of God on behalf of someone else.

Not long ago, our church was going through some difficult times and I sent a message to the intercession team. I said, "All of you who are on that team, if you are not for this ministry succeeding then please dismiss yourself." Some in the group became upset and wanted to meet with me and I refused because the message was plain and clear. Basically, what I was saying is that we have to be careful about who we have interceding for us.

There are some people who will go into the Prayer Room and start praying against us instead of for us. It's not that I doubted the people on the intercession team, but I had to make the message clear.

Abigail calls Nabal a fool for what he did, but when she went to intercede for him and bring this gift to the king, she offers to take the blame. Even though she was "hooked up" to a fool, she did not allow his foolish ways to turn her heart to a place where she lost her sense of love and mercy. We can't let other's actions change the person that God has made us to be. Abigail refused to allow Nabal's foolishness to transform her into some plastic, hard-nosed, hard core, and uncaring individual. She kept the love that God had given her. She refused to allow her circumstances to change who she really was. She still had enough love to pray the right kind of prayer. She could have said, "David, I'm tired of this Nabal. Take my gift and spare me but do me a favor and take that fool out." God is looking at how we handle our situation and handle our surroundings. He wants to know if we are going to be like God in our situation.

"Now, my lord, as surely as the LORD lives and you yourself live, since the LORD has kept you from murdering and taking vengeance into your own hands, let all your enemies and those who try to harm you be as cursed as Nabal is. And here is a present that I, your servant, have brought to you and your young men." **(1 Samuel 25:26-27 TLB)**

When Abigail interceded, she makes her prayer king–centered and not Nabal-centered. In other words, she reminded the king that she knew who he was. Anybody who knows something about prayer and interceding knows that one of the greatest and quickest ways you can get to God is just by reminding Him that we know who He is! There is something about interceding and praying the promises of God and telling Him we have not forgotten who He is that releases power in our lives. God wants to know if we really believe He is who He says He is. God wants to hear it from each of us.

"Please forgive me if I have offended you in any way. The LORD will surely reward you with a lasting dynasty, for you are fighting the LORD's battles. And you have not done wrong throughout your entire life. Even when you are chased by those who seek to kill you, your life is safe in the care of the LORD your God, secure in his treasure pouch! But the lives of your enemies will disappear like stones shot from a sling! When the LORD has done all he promised and has made you leader of Israel, don't let this be a blemish on your record. Then your conscience won't have to bear the staggering burden of needless bloodshed and vengeance. And when the LORD has done these great things for you, please remember me, your servant!" **(1 Samuel 25:28-31 TLB)**

Abigail used good judgment as she skillfully and humbly reminded David who he was. David realized that this wise woman had indeed prevented him from doing something that went against all that he was trying to stand for.

David said to Abigail, "Praise be to the LORD, the God of Israel, who has sent you today to meet me. May you be blessed for your **good judgment** and for keeping me from bloodshed this day and from avenging myself with my own hands. Otherwise, as surely as the LORD, the God of Israel, lives, who has kept me from harming you, if you had not come quickly to meet me, not one male belonging to Nabal would have been left alive by daybreak." (1 Samuel 25:32-34)

## Let the King Be the King

Then David accepted from her hand what she had brought him and said, "Go home in peace. I have heard your words and granted your request." **(1 Samuel 25:35 NIV)**

David accepted from her hand what she had brought him and granted her request. She interceded to the king and brought the king her best. If Abigail and David had done the wrong thing here, they would have missed out receiving the blessing that God had down the road for them with a clear conscience. Instead of doing their own thing, they allowed God to be God. They approached this situation with "a hands off" policy. There are some things that God wants us to handle and take care of. However, there are some things that we've got to look at, measure, and trust God by simply taking our hands knowing that God is able to handle it.

If we refuse to take our hands off, we are only going to make the situation worse. When we put our hands on these things, we are in essence saying to God, "I do not trust You to handle this situation. I'm going to handle it myself." When we take these particular things into our own hands, we cause God to take His hands off it. We actually keep His hands from moving in our particular situation. There are times when we've just got to relax and just let God be God and realize that the battle is not ours, it is the Lord's.

Do not repay anyone evil for evil. Be careful to do what is right in the eyes of everyone. If it is possible, as far as it depends on you, live at peace with everyone. Do not take revenge, my dear friends, but leave room for God's wrath, for it is written: "It is mine to avenge; I will repay," says the Lord. **(Romans 12:17-19 NIV)**

This tells us that when we find ourselves in these situations that our job is to do three things: (1) Do not repay evil for evil, (2) do what is right, and (3) live peaceably if it is possible.

After David blessed her, Abigail goes back home and gets ready to talk to her husband to inform him of her interactions with the king. When she arrived home, Nabal was engaged in a party and was drunk. She waited until the next morning and told Nabal what had taken place. When she told him these things, his heart died within him. It became as a stone. About ten days after that, the Lord smote Nabal, and he died **(1 Samuel 25:36-42)**. If David had done it there would have been blood on his hands. If

Abigail had told him to do it or allowed him to do it, she would have been living with guilt and unable to enjoy what God had down the road for her. She did the right thing. She let God handle it.

Because both Abigail and David responded correctly, David was free to love Abigail and take her as his wife after Nabal died! He could marry her with a free conscience. He could do it without his reputation being stained. He was still able to receive a blessing because he allowed God to be God. She was able to be blessed because she allowed God to be God!

### Key Points:

- Don't let other's actions change the person God has made us to be.
- We keep His hands from moving in our particular situation.
- We need to take our hands off so God can handle it.
- "It is mine to avenge; I will repay," says the Lord.
- Let God be God for the battle is the Lord's.
- Do not repay anyone evil for evil.
- Live at peace with everyone.
- Always give God our best.
- Don't take revenge.
- God handled it!

**Ask Yourself:**

1. Am I releasing my praise to God so He can start moving on my behalf?
2. Am I bringing my gift before my king?
3. Am I allowing my circumstances to change who I am?
4. Do I have joy in the midst of struggle?

**Declare:**

"God, look at my situation. I believe when You promised to be a friend, you meant it for me. I believe when You promised to be a counselor, you would do that for me. I believe when You said that Your mercy endures forever, that applies to my situation right now. I believe when You said that by Your stripes, I am healed that I am healed. I believe when You said you would never allow anything to come upon my life that I won't have the power to bear, You would be there to bear it with me. I believe when You promised to make a way out when I could not see it, that You are doing that in my life right now."

# SECTION SIX

# DAVID

May the spirit of a "recoverer" overcome you. May it release that warrior spirit within you as you rise up and take back everything that the enemy has stolen from you.

## *Warrior in Recovery*

And David inquired of the Lord, shall I pursue after this troop? Shall I overtake them? And he answered him, pursue: for thou shalt surely overtake them, and without fail recover all. (1 Samuel 30:8)

The 1960s and 1970s were considered to be turbulent times for America as it found itself shaken by the many crises that would arise during this scary and trying decade. The nation had seen its beloved President John F. Kennedy assassinated in his motorcade in Dallas, Texas on November 22, 1963. Then just five years later, perhaps the greatest civil rights leader who ever lived, the Rev. Martin Luther King, Jr. was also assassinated as he stood on the balcony of his hotel in Memphis, Tennessee on April 4, 1968. About the time the nation could catch its breath, Robert F.

Kennedy, the brother of John F. Kennedy, was gunned down in Washington D. C. on June 5, 1968.

To go along with all of this bloodshed of national figures, the nation was also embroiled in what can only be described as a military quagmire that came to be known as the Vietnam War. This war that seemed to lead to nowhere drew protests from national leaders such as Dr. King, as well as the nation's youth who expressed their outrage in the forms of sit-ins, marches, campus protests, and many other forms in an attempt to communicate to the government the need to bring their soldiers back home from war. One of the many of protests came in the form of music that expressed a hatred of this particular conflict as well as a hatred for war itself. One of the songs during the day was a song that was written by Edwin Stair that became a political anthem that rose to the top of the music charts during the long hot summer of 1970. The song was simply entitled "War." The lyrics of the main part of that song basically went, "War, good God, what is it good for? Absolutely nothing!"

Now during the time in which they were living, I can understand the passion behind such lyrics and the desire to avoid war at all costs. But let me say that I cannot totally agree with the lyrics of this song. For this journey called living has taught me that there comes a time in every life where war is absolutely necessary. **Ecclesiastes 1:1-8** says that there is a season, a time, and a purpose for everything under heaven. Then in verse 4 it says there is a time to love, a time to hate, a time of war, and a time of peace. There comes a time when one discovers that there are things in life that are so dear and are of such intrinsic value that they are worth fighting for. Regardless how passive you may be, when you are backed in a corner and your convictions are being challenged, you will eventually have to stand up and fight.

It is for that reason that God has imbedded within the fabric of every human being a warrior spirit. A spirit designed to give us the fight and the motivation to make it through the battles and wars of life that we find ourselves engaged in from time to time. There are battles with demoniac forces, battles with our flesh, financial battles, battles for the family, battles for our marriage, battles to obtain justice and battles that determine our destiny. God has placed that warrior spirit in us that enables us to be able to stand and be successful during the battles of life. There is a warrior inside of each of us!

We need to know that because without proper recognition of this spirit, one will find themselves quickly defeated by life's issues and relegated to being a victimized bystander, sitting on the sidelines watching life pass them by. Without knowing that warrior spirit, one would be prone to give up at the mere sight of opposition, and have one's destiny hindered, aborted, and deterred. Without knowing the warrior spirit, one becomes a pushover or a wimp in life constantly being bullied by the devil or even some other person. It is that warrior spirit on the inside that causes us to rise up from the mat where we've been knocked down. It is that warrior spirit in us that makes us get out of bed when depression is trying to hold us there and have a pity party. It is that warrior spirit which decides that regardless of how dark the night and how long the days, we are going to hang in there until God gives us the victory.

It is that warrior spirit that helps us recognize that in spite of our circumstances, we are more than conquerors through Him that loves us. There's a warrior inside each of us! The best thing for a Christian who is full of destiny to do is to get to know that warrior spirit within and when and how it's supposed to be used. There are few things more destructive than a person whose warrior spirit within is out of control because they live life in a constant state of conflict with other people. They'll fight when they do not need to fight and live with their guard up in such a way that they actually hurt the very people that are trying to love them. They push away and fight against the people that are trying to help them.

On the other hand, there's nothing more pathetic than a man or a woman who has not discovered their warrior spirit and does not know how to use it. The devil prowls around pillaging and plundering whenever he chooses, working out his three-fold plan to kill, steal, and destroy. Once we realize that God has put that warrior spirit on the inside of us and that it is designed to stand up to and do battle with demon forces, we can be victorious in life. Regardless of one's background, financial situation, or position in life, we need to realize that God has placed a warrior spirit inside us so we can be victorious. We've got the victory!

## David had a Warrior Spirit

There are only a few men in Scripture that embody the spirit of a warrior like the star of this book, David. Yet to be Israel's greatest king, the former stone-slinging shepherd who stepped from the lowly sheepfold on to the stage of history with the courage of the lion and the accuracy of a skilled marksman, David was a worshipper and a warrior. He was a man who could dance before the Lord with all his might, and then get angry enough to gather an army together and slay 100,000 men. David could sit on a hillside and pen the words of Scripture's most heartfelt Psalms, and at the same time possess the rugged passion and strength that made him known as the nation's greatest warrior. David always seemed to be in the right place at the right time and always one step ahead of the devil.

However, in **1 Samuel 30:8** it would appear that the enemy had won because he struck at a time when David and his troops seemed to be at the wrong place at the wrong time. David is in a pressure-filled, awkward position. He is a fugitive fleeing from King Saul, and he is also avoiding the Philistines who have been his enemy for many years. He found a haven of safety in a place called Ziklag and, as usual, his anointed leadership and warrior skills served to thrust him into the forefront.

As the story unfolds David and his troops are returning from some military campaigns and no doubt, they are looking forward to seeing their loving wives and having their children running into their arms. As they drew near to their home, they find tragedy awaiting them. Their vision of anticipation is broken as the stench of a burned down and ruined city reaches their nostrils. Fearing the worse these valiant warriors approached their city only to find that their women and their children had been taken captive and the city had been burned to the ground. It is here in the midst of tragedy and loss that David leads his men down the road to recovery and the heart of a true warrior is revealed.

# CHAPTER 10

# THE FIVE "RS" ON THE ROAD TO RECOVERY – RECOGNIZE, RELEASE, REFOCUS, REQUEST, RECOVER

We want to examine this story and see the steps that David, the warrior in recovery, took to lead his men on the road to recovery and snatch victory out of the jaws of defeat. There are five steps that David took on this road to recovery.

### Recognize Who the Enemy Really Is

It came to pass when David and his men were come to Ziklag and on the third day that the Amalekites had invaded from the South and had smitten Ziklag and burned it with fire. **(1 Samuel 30:1)**

When it comes to fighting, we cannot waste precious time fighting the wrong enemies and fail to recognize the real nature of what we are up against.

The Amalakites were David's enemies in this incident. Who were they? According to historians, the Amalekites, were a group of marauders who were descendants of Esau's grandson, Amalek. They had been the arch enemies of Israel since the days of Moses. God had instructed Moses in Deuteronomy 25:17-19 to do battle against the Amalakites in a specific way. Basically, God told them, "Not only do I want you to defeat the Amalekites but I literally want you to go down and wipe them off the face of the earth." God told Moses to annihilate the Amalekites because they worshipped false gods. Instead of dealing with the Amalakites as God had told them to, they allowed them to remain on the earth. We find Gideon having to fight them in the book of Judges. King Saul was ordered to fight them and to wipe them out during his time as King, but Saul refused to do it as well.

Now David has to deal with an enemy that should have been annihilated generations ago. This generational curse had been passed on from generation to generation. Many of us have to deal with generational curses that have been passed down through our families as well. We need to understand that the battles we are confronting on a daily basis may not be about us or our generation. Often times we are fighting for future generations because any time a giant is allowed to remain among us, our children and children's children will have to deal with it sometime in the future. That's why we talked about dealing with any Goliath in our lives in book one. We've got to come to a point where we realize there are certain things we cannot afford to let stay. We've got to rise up with our warrior spirit and decide that enough is enough! God has given us the power! He has armed and anointed us for such a time as this.

## Release Emotional Distress

So, when David and his men came to the city, and, behold, it was burned with fire; and their wives, and their sons, and their daughters, were taken captives. Then David and the people that were with him lifted up their voices and wept, until they had no more power to weep. **(1 Samuel 30:3-4)**

One of the leading causes of most of our physical ailments is stress. Stress will kill us if we are not careful. It has a way of eating us up on the inside. As a matter of fact, someone once said, "It is not what we eat that kills us but what we allow to eat us." There's both outward stress which we cannot control, and there's inward stress that we need to learn how to release. One of the blessed outlets that God has given us is the vehicle called emotional release. Talk to somebody who can be trusted. Screaming sometimes helps us let it out. Exercise, a good laugh, or a good old-fashioned cry can offer release of emotional distress. Pride and stereotyping are obstacles to emotional release, especially for men. A real man doesn't cry is a lie that will keep us in bondage to emotional distress. We need to understand that men and women are emotional, and both can suffer from emotional distress. We just express differently for we have been conditioned to manage our emotions in almost opposite ways. The truth is real men do cry. As a matter of fact, one of the reasons why women outlive men is because they are more in touch with their emotions, and they release their stress through tears.

Notice what these season, strong and rugged soldiers do when they come back to their city and find it burned to the ground and their women and children missing. These warriors understood that skillful battle is not done in a spirit of anger and pent-up emotional rage. No one can fight properly if they are fighting out of anger. That kind of leader will end up destroying people and things. So, upon seeing the tragedy these strong fighting men wept out loud until they had no strength left to weep.

Weep in your father's arms when grief and pain threaten to overwhelm you. Tell Him it's too much, you cannot take it anymore. Bring your complaint and weep before the Lord. David and his troop realized they could not do battle if they were pent up with rage. David wrote in Psalm 30:5, "Weeping may remain for a night, but rejoicing comes in the morning" (NIV). Go someplace and release that grief and pain. Let it go!

### Re-focus

"David was greatly distressed···But David found strength in the Lord his God. **(1 Samuel 30:6 NIV)**

The thing that we have to admire about David and the process of recovery he is exemplifying for us is that he knew that in order for him to lead he first had to deal with his own mind-set. We don't want anybody leading us who doesn't have his own head together. We need somebody that will get alone with God and get their own head together first before they start giving orders.

David was greatly distressed and was a man under a great deal of pressure. because after seeing the tragedy the men David was fighting with seemed to be searching for a scapegoat. They focused their attention on David, their leader and the foreigner, and the scripture says the men sought to stone him. Along with that David's family was missing as well so he was grieving along with his soldiers. But as a man in touch with his emotions, instead of getting discouraged and having a pity party; David encouraged himself and found strength in the Lord, his God. There are times when we all will have to encourage ourselves in the Lord.

We've got to minister to ourselves sometimes. We've got to pick ourselves up and get re-focused on the Lord our God.

David was a worshipper so in the process of refocusing, he sends for Abiathar, the priest's son, and said, "Bring me hither the ephod" (1 Samuel 30:7). The ephod was a spiritual or religious garment that the priests would wear for a season of celebration. Every time they got ready to celebrate, priests would come and put on the linen ephod as a symbol of victory. Their wives and children were missing, and the city had been burned down, but David said, "I've got to refocus. I've got to get my focus back. I've encouraged myself but before I take another step, I need to get the linen ephod and I need to celebrate. I've got to praise my God."

David said, "I will bless the Lord at all times. His praise shall continually be in my mouth" **(Psalm 34:1)**. At all times, in the good times and in the bad times; when we're up and when we're down, we've got to bless the name of the Lord, for He is worthy to be praised.

"O magnify the Lord with me and let us exalt His name together" **(Psalm 34:3 AMP)**. Sometimes as children, we would get those little magnifying glasses so we could clearly see the little bugs. One of the things a magnifying glass would do would help you to focus better. If you want to see how something unclear becomes clearer, you look through the magnifying glass. Refocusing by magnifying and worshipping the Lord helps us see God as bigger than our problem. We need to learn how to magnify God because when we magnify Him, our battles become small and our God becomes big. He'll stand by us. The battle belongs to the Lord. Magnify the Lord!

### Make Your Request Known to the King

David inquired of the Lord, "Shall I pursue this raiding party? Will I overtake them?" **(1 Samuel 30:8a NIV)**

David had learned from all of his many experiences with the Lord, that God always has the plan. If God said go then it was time to go. If God said wait, it was time to wait. If God said no then they were not to go. David inquired of the Lord. God's way always brings the victory though it may not always be the way we thought it would be achieved. David was willing to do things God's way. He also knew that although he was a warrior with a warrior spirit that the key to that spirit being constructive as opposed to destructive was submitting to Gods divine direction.

He did not want to engage in the practice of simply fighting battles but wanted to make sure that the battles he fought were under the direction of God.

## Recover It All

"Pursue them," [the Lord] answered. "You will certainly overtake them and succeed in the rescue." **(1 Samuel 30:8b NIV)**

David and his troops get a command from God. When we get clearance from God to go, God will provide a way to find out who and where the enemy shelters and feeds. David did not have a clue where the Amalakites had taken their families, but God said go so David and six hundred men rose up and travelled to the Bezor ravine. They ran into an Egyptian boy who was one of the slaves of the Amalakites. He had been there for three days without food and without water. The Bible says that they gave him a fig cake and water and when he was revived, they asked him if he knew where the Amalekite army had gone.

When we get directions from God, He will not only tell us what to do but He'll show us the way to get it done. When we have submitted to the will of God, He will direct our path. "Trust in the Lord with all thine heart and lean not unto thine own understanding. In all thy ways acknowledge Him and He will direct your path" **(Proverbs 3:5-6)**. **Psalms 37:23** says, "The steps of a good man are ordered by the Lord." In other words, God will not only guide us but He also will provide all that we need to get the victory.

God used the Egyptian slave boy to lead David and his men right to where the Amalekites were eating, drinking, and dancing over the spoil that they had taken out of Ziklag. David and his troops rose up, fought against the Amalekites, and recovered all that the Amalekites had carried away. There was nothing lacking to them neither small nor great; neither sons nor daughters; neither spoil nor anything that was taken from them. David recovered it all (1 Samuel 30:18-20).

### Key Points:

- Magnify God - our battles become small and our God becomes big.
- Rise up and recover everything that the enemy has taken.
- God is awakening that warrior spirit on the inside.
- We need to re-focus on the Lord our God.
- There is a warrior inside each of us!
- We've got to pick ourselves up!
- We've got the victory!
- Magnify the Lord!
- Arise Warrior!

### Ask Yourself:

1. What issues do I need to deal with that I have accepted into my life and my family?
2. Do I bless the name of the Lord when I'm up and when I'm down?

3. Do I recognize who my enemy really is?

4. Do I have a way to release my emotional stress?

5. Have I made my requests known to the Lord?

6. Am I ready to take back all that the enemy has stolen?

**Declare:**

"I'm sick and tired of being sick and tired! I'm going to rise up out of this negative situation. I am more than a conqueror! I am the apple of God's eye. I'm anointed and appointed. I'm the top and not the bottom, the head and not the tail. I'm victorious. I've got power. I'm blessed. It's recovery time!

I am taking back my joy! I am taking back my power! I am taking back my blessing! I am taking back my community! I am taking back my children and grandchildren! It's recovery time!"

# CONCLUSION

# DAVID

How do you know when you are ready to reign? You love and fear God more than anything else. You are faithful in small beginnings, and you've learned to respond properly to your enemies. You are ready for increase!

## Ready to Reign

So, all the elders of Israel came to the King to Hebron; and King David made a league with them in Hebron before the Lord; and they anointed him David king over Israel. **(2 Samuel 5:3)**

It is within the divine will and desire of Almighty God to bring us all to a place of preparedness. In His divine wisdom God is constantly working in and through events to bring all of us to a point in which we find ourselves prepared for our next place of assignment. He desires that when the time for our destined place comes that we walk into that place not lacking anything that is necessary for our assured success.

My brethren, count it all joy when you fall into diverse temptations, knowing this, that the trying of your faith worketh patience, but let patience have her perfect work that ye may be perfect and entire wanting nothing. **(James 1:2-4)**

In other words, James was saying that every time we go through something, every place that God leads us, and everything that He allows to happen is part of His divine plan. It is part of the master plan of the Father to aid in our development, add something to our stature, build our character, add to our spiritual résumé, and equip us for the place where He desires us to reign.

Like a master chef preparing a great feast, God sprinkles in some trials, puts a dash of good times, a dash of bad times, and mixes it with some temptations. He places us in the oven called the furnace of affliction while protecting us with the grace of staying power. He transports us on to the mountain of inspiration and down into the valley of revelation. He let us experience the loneliness of the wilderness and the pain of the lion's den and the fiery furnace where we have to decide to make a stand for Him. All of these events and destinations are preparing us to reach our place of destiny. Regardless of where we find ourselves, we need to understand that everything we go through and everywhere we go is all part of the Master Plan. The ups and downs are part of the Plan. The painful and inconsistent relationship is part of the plan, that overbearing boss on the job is part of the Plan. It is all a part of the Plan to complete and prepare us for our next assignment. It's all part of God's Master Plan!

**One of the ways in which we can know the difference between a God-appointment and a man-appointment is found in this issue of readiness.**

Even when I don't understand it, it's all just part of the Plan! God desires that when we go into our next appointment that we are prepared and needing absolutely nothing. One of the ways in which we can know the difference between a God-appointment and a man-appointment is found in this issue of readiness. Mankind will try to promote someone to a place based on their own desire and selfish motives. God will never place anyone in a place for which they are not ready. God will not only divinely appoint He will also divinely anoint. Real anointing can only be obtained through the pain, the tedium, and the places that are involved in this thing called process.

It makes no difference who you are or who you might be connected to; you'll never get anointed until you go through the process. You cannot order it from your favorite Tele-Evangelist. You cannot send away and have it delivered for $19.95 by dialing an 800 number. You cannot obtain it by going to the Fire and Tongues University or by getting a diploma from a professor. No, it can only be experienced by paying the price through God ordained process because the Anointing is expensive and is going to cost you something far beyond money. Only the God of heaven who examines the heart and the spirit of a person is the One who decides who He is going to anoint and who can be trusted with the anointing.

In order to determine if we are ready reign under His anointing, He takes us to places and He brings us through tests and trials. He lets us experience some pain and some rejection along the way. He allows us to feel the wind and the rain, and the storms of life to test whether or not we're really going to trust Him. He brings us to places in which our integrity is going to be tested in order to find out if we come with a price tag. He takes us to places where we have to stand up for what is right no matter what it's going to cost us. God brings us to these places to test us and see if we can be trusted with an anointing.

God takes us through these things in order to prepare us for the next place of assignment. We will never get there until we go through the process. We cannot skip the process because if we do, we'll find we are in an office in which we are not qualified to speak out of. We'll find we are speaking out of books as opposed to speaking out of experience. Never skip the process!

At the halfway point of David's life, he has reached the place God has been preparing him for from his teen years. God brought characters into David's life preparing him for this moment in time. There was Jesse the father who overlooked him, Eliab the brother playa-hater, Samuel the Prophet who laid his hands on him, Goliath the giant who came to make or break him, Saul to bring out his best, Jonathan to be his covenant friend, Ahimelech and Abiathar who were friends without a price tag, and Abigail who was hooked up to a fool but full of wisdom and sound judgment.

David has progressed from a warrior in recovery to the fulfillment of the prophecy that began David's journey—the ceremony marking the crowning and the anointing of a king! David had finally made it. After going through everything that he went through he was finally ready to walk into his place of destiny and reign in his place of appointment.

How did David know he was ready for this event? How do we know when we're ready to walk into the place God has for us? I believe there are four simple indicators about David that will help us understand whether we are ready to reign.

### 1. When you love and fear God more than anything else.

For the eyes of the Lord run to and fro throughout the whole earth to show himself strong on the behalf of those whose heart is perfect toward him. **(2 Chronicles 16:9)**

God referred to David as a man after His own heart. This is a person whose life is in harmony with God. They have such a relationship with God that what is important to God becomes important to them. They hate what God hates and love what God loves. What burdens God ends up burdening them. When God says go right, they are willing to go right. When He says go left, they are willing to go left. When he says stop something, they stop. When He says something is wrong, they walk away from it. That's how a man knows they are a person after God's own heart.

In John 14:15 Jesus said, "If you love Me, you're going to keep My commandments." You don't care who's watching you. Your response is not based on whether the pastor is around or if he is absent. Nobody has to beg you to be obedient to God. If you really love Him there's something on the inside of you that's going to cause you to want to please Him.

In **Mark 12:29-31** Jesus said, "The first of all the commandments is, Hear, O Israel; the Lord our God is one Lord: And thou shalt love the Lord thy God with all thy soul, and with all thy mind, and with all thy strength: this is the first commandment. And the second is like, namely this, thou shalt love they neighbor as thyself. There is none other commandment greater than these."

Do you love everybody and not just those who treat you right? Are you able to love your enemies? Are you able to love those who are talking about you and criticizing you and calling you everything but a child of God? When you really love Jesus, you don't have a choice in the matter. There's just something on the inside that just can't allow you to walk in hate, in malice, and in vengeance. I'm talking about a person who has a heart after God. I'm talking about a person who really loves Jesus. There's something on the inside that will cause you to love everybody.

If there's somebody whose opinion you fear more than God and that you love more than God that is idolatry and you're not ready to reign anywhere. The reason God chose David is because God knew that David loved Him and wanted Him more than he wanted a kingdom.

God chose David because He knew that once David was promoted and blessed, he was not going to forget that if it had not been for the Lord that was on his side he would never have been blessed, promoted, and delivered. He would never have been a giant killer. The Bible says that God is a rewarder of them that diligently seek Him. If you want to know how to be blessed, seek first the Kingdom of God and His righteousness and all of these things shall be added unto you.

As the deer panteth after the water brook so panteth my soul after thee, O God. **(Psalm 42:1)**.

## 2. When you have been faithful in small beginnings.

You are never going to reach your place of destiny and reign there until you've been faithful in the area in which God has you right now. It is interesting how we want to be promoted to positions of significance when we are not even faithful in the place we are right now. If you're going to be promoted and you're going to reign, you've got to be faithful in the places of small beginnings. That's the thing about David. David was a shepherd boy doing a job that nobody else wanted to do. All the young men dreamed about being warriors, being in the army, and being captains, but David was sent to do a thankless job of watching, shearing, feeding, protecting, and rescuing the sheep.

David was able to look at the thing that he did and compare it to the faithfulness and nature of his God as it shows us in **Psalm 23**, "The Lord is my Shepherd, and I shall not want." David understood a principle that simply says, "You can walk in a lowly position, get anointed, and use the gifts that God has given you to make that lowly position something that everybody wants."

At every level that God has blessed me to labor in His Kingdom, I tried to take that assignment run as far as I could with it. When I taught my Sunday School class, I made that class the place to be. When I ran the maintenance team, everybody wanted to be on the maintenance team. When I sang in the group everybody wanted to sing in the group because we did everything that we did with a spirit of excellence. When I served National Evangelist, I tried to do it with fervor and with passion. I attempted to be faithful as all levels.

In order for God to elevate you to the next level, you've got to be so committed that whether folks are watching you or ignoring you, you've got to have the mind-set that says, "I'm going to do everything that I do for God with a spirit of excellence. I'm going to develop myself. I'm not going to despise the day of small beginnings. I'm going to be faithful where I am." When God sees that kind of faithfulness, He is willing and ready to promote us to the next level.

In **Luke 19:17** Jesus said, "Because you were faithful over little things, I will give you authority over ten cities." He is willing and ready to promote us to the next level. This man had been faithful where he was so God moved him to the next level. What you are doing may seem insignificant, but if you'll be faithful right where you are, God will promote you to another level. God will open up a door that no man can shut. He'll know that you're ready to reign when you've been faithful over small beginnings.

**Anytime you respond to your enemies the same way Saul does, you are telling God that once you arrive at the place of power you're going to be just like Saul.**

### 3. When you respond properly to your enemies.

From the time David received his anointing and a prophetic word from Samuel, his enemies came to the forefront. Some of them had already been there but they were hiding. Some of them were new, created by what I can only call prophetic success. He was anointed saying that he was going to be the next king and his enemies came out of nowhere based on what God told him he was going to be. He had people angry at him when all he had was a prophecy. That's what the enemy will try to do. He will try to cut you off before your prophetic word can come to pass.

Notice David's response to his enemies. There was his own brother Eliab whose words were designed to discourage him. David ignored him. His father Jesse failed to recognize him. David turned to God. The giant wanted to kill him and threatened all Israel. David took him out. The hardest test for David was how he was to respond to Saul. Saul was God's anointed. Still in his God-given position! David respected him and allowed God to take care of the situation.

Every one of us who are called to reign are going to be confronted by a Saul, somebody who does not like you based on how you do what you do because you're anointed. Saul kept a jealous eye on David. If David had not responded correctly, he would have had to go through the test all over again. David was blessed because though he had to go through the wilderness and difficult times, David refused to stoop to the level of Saul. He still honored Saul as God's anointed even when he had the opportunity to take him out. He still showed love. Therefore, God was able to promote him.

Anytime you respond to your enemies the same way Saul does, you are telling God that once you arrive at the place of power you're going to be just like Saul. When you are mature enough to realize that Saul is just being a tool of the demonic spirit that was tormenting him and mature enough to know that regardless of what Saul is doing you are going to do what is right, you are ready to reign God's way. That person that is coming up against you is just an instrument of the enemy so instead of getting filled with hatred toward Saul, your boss, and everybody else that's coming against you, direct your anger at the enemy of your soul.

David had knowledge that enabled him to love those who were still trying to kill him. David understood that if he did the right thing, God would take care of Saul. Some people stay up all night trying to figure to how out how to get back at their enemies. In Luke 6:27-28 Jesus said, "Love your enemies, do good to them that hate you, bless them that curse you, and pray for them that despitefully use you." We've got to respond properly to our enemies because our promotion and our place of destiny is depending on our response.

**Charles Swindoll has said, "Oftentimes we are better at handling affliction than we are at handling promotion."**

### 4. When you are ready for increase.

Anointing is a strange thing! It's one of those things that you can have but also one of those things which you can never get enough of. We are to continue to grow in it. However, one is never ready for an increase in the Kingdom until they have done something with the anointing which they already have. God doesn't anoint lazy people. When we are busy for God and there is a demand on our anointing, God gives us more to meet the demand. God anoints those who are active and those who are willing to go out and meet the needs of His people.

What is the anointing? It is the supernatural ability to do business for God. It is basically the presence of God on the life of an individual. There are specific anointing's for different tasks, and the greater the task, the greater the anointing.

In biblical times, kings were anointed as a symbol that God had stamped His approval upon their appointment. David was anointed at the house of Jesse. He wasn't anointed for where he was but he was anointed for where he was going. The anointing was designed to take him from the sheepfold to the throne. Therefore, he was anointed to deal with rejection. He was anointed to deal with his brothers hating him. He was anointed to deal with the giant, Goliath. He was anointed to deal with and recover everything that the enemy had taken. He was anointed to get from Point A to Point B.

When he arrives at Point B, David is about to enter into a new level of reigning. He had walked in one anointing to get him there but now what he needed was a **kingly anointing.** This anointing was not just designed to get him there but was designed to keep him there once he got there. Charles Swindoll has said, "Oftentimes we are better at handling affliction than we are at handling promotion". In essence what Charles Swindoll is saying is that there are some folks who are fine as long as they are struggling. There are some people who are faithful to God and are fine as long as they are at the bottom looking up. But as soon as God blesses them with a little something, as soon as they get the promotion and a level of financial or career success, all of a sudden, they forget about the God who has blessed them and brought them there.

David had the right mind-set he said, "Yes, I was anointed at the house of Jesse! Yes, I knew that somehow, someway, God was going to get me here. But now that I'm here, I need something more. I don't want to be like Saul and get on the throne and forget who promoted me there. I don't want to be like Saul and lose my anointing and try to rule by intimidation and fear. I don't want to be like Saul and end up visiting the witch at Endor. I want You to anoint me God so that I can stay in this place. It took the anointing to get me here. Now, I need an anointing to keep me

# BIBLIOGRAPHY

Edwards, Gene "A Tale of Three Kings" Tyndale House Publishers Inc Carol Stream, Illinois. copyright 1980.

Swindoll, Charles "David- A Man of Passion and Destiny" Word Publishing, Dallas, Texas copyright 1997.

Ryken, Leland. "Dictionary of Biblical Imagery" Inter Varsity Press. Downers Grove, Illinois. Copyright 1998

Comay, Joan. "Who's who in the Bible" Wings Books. New York 1980

Websters New World Dictionary 3rd College Edition Copyright 1988

Spiros, Zodhiates. "The Complete Word Study Dictionary AMG publishers Chattanooga, Tennessee 1992

Vine, W.E. Vine Expository Dictionary of Old and New Testament Thomas Nelson Publishers 1985

Lockyer, Herbert. "All The Kings and Queens of the Bible" Zondervan Publishing House. Grand Rapids, Michigan 1961

To Order books and Products from Lee Ministries visit our website at: www.leeministries.org.

For bookings and other information contact us at wleemin@aol.com